MEDICAL ASPECTS OF
FITNESS TO DRIVE

A guide for Medical Practitioners

Editor: Dr J.F. Taylor CBE FRCP FFOM

Published by
The Medical Commission on Accident Prevention

35–43 Lincoln's Inn Fields
London WC2A 3PN
Telephone: 0171 242 3176

CONTENTS

Page

FOREWORD

KENSINGTON PALACE
LONDON W8

The number of motorists using our roads continues to increase. As a keen driver myself, I am glad to see that the medical profession are keeping themselves informed about this important subject. Many outside the profession will also find this book useful and informative and I am sure it will attract many readers overseas.

The work that has been done on the medical aspects of road safety over the last ten years has been impressive. I congratulate the Commission for this comprehensive, concise and readable volume.

President, The Medical Commission on Accident Prevention.

INTRODUCTION

By the Editor: Dr John Taylor CBE FRCP FFOM

It is ten years since the previous edition which proved a great success with the distribution of some 70,000 copies worldwide. It is with some trepidation and humility that I step into the shoes of Dr Andrew Raffle, whose successful editorship of earlier editions of this booklet has been widely applauded. In those ten years since the previous edition, there have been many scientific developments in the field of traffic medicine as well as in legislation, largely dominated by the second European Community directive for a common community driving licence which is effective from July 1996.

Throughout this edition, distinction is made between Group I drivers medical standards (motorcyclists and car and Light Goods Vehicle drivers) and Group II which is applied to Goods Vehicle drivers driving vehicles in excess of 3.5 metric tonnes laden weight and bus drivers and coach drivers (See Chapter 2 Part I). By convention, Group II standards are also generally applied to emergency police, firemen and ambulance drivers as well as taxi drivers.

Since the last edition of the booklet, all British driving licences are now issued by the Driver and Vehicle Licensing Centre. Patients notifying disabilities during the currency of a driving licence should write to the **Medical Adviser, Drivers Medical Unit, DVLA, Longview Road, Swansea, SA99 1TU. Doctors wishing to discuss cases with a medical adviser at the Licensing Centre should telephone 01792 783686.**

A recent tragedy involved a 19 year old, killed by a driver with Alzheimer's disease who was driving the wrong way up the M62 motorway. Where a patients disorder makes him manifestly dangerous as a driver and his condition renders him incapable of taking advice that he must inform DVLA or where he refuses to do so practitioners

5

have a civil law duty to immediately inform DVLA medical staff. To do so is acting within the General Medical Council's guidance but practitioners must be prepared to defend their decision.

My thanks are due to the individual Chapter Authors, Members of the Secretary of State's Honorary Medical Advisory Panels on Driving and to Dr Rowse and her team of DVLA Medical Advisers as well as members of the Transport Committee of the Commission.

The tabulated summaries at the end of chapters were first published as the "At a Glance" booklet and are attributed to the painstaking work of Dr John Irvine. Readers will find these valuable for quick reference when advising patients. Unless otherwise stated in these the applicant/ driving licence holder needs to report the medical condition to DVLA.

1

PREVALENCE OF MEDICAL FACTORS IN ROAD TRAFFIC ACCIDENTS

By the Editor: John Taylor CBE FRCP FFOM*

The available evidence suggests that medical conditions of drivers with the exception of the effects of alcohol, are not an important factor in road accidents causing injury to other road users. Most road traffic accidents have a multi-factorial cause. On the spot studies in the UK[1] and USA,[2] have shown that approximately 95 per cent of RTAs have human factor involvement (Figure 1) but only about one hospital admission accident in 250 has an associated medical factor.

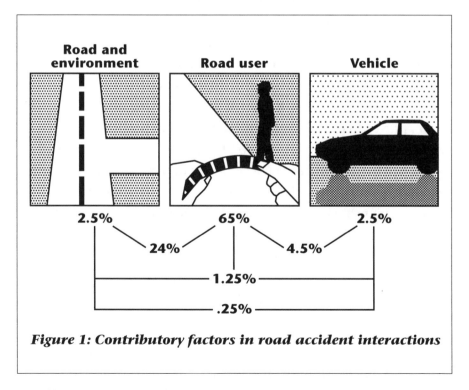

Figure 1: Contributory factors in road accident interactions

*   *Chairman Transport Committee, Medical Commission on Accident Prevention.*

PREVALENCE OF MEDICAL FACTORS
IN ROAD TRAFFIC ACCIDENTS

Figure 2 (opposite) shows the ranking order of medical factor accidents. Overall generalised tonic clonic (grand mal) *epilepsy* features in approximately 39 per cent of medical factor road traffic accidents with *insulin injectors* being involved in 17 per cent, but *heart attacks*, which account for over 40 per cent of UK deaths, are a factor in only ten per cent (Figure 2). The relatively low incidence rate in contrast to the high morbidity of potentially significant medical conditions in the Community is difficult to explain, and this is particularly notable in regard to visual deficits. *Vision* is the primary sensory input required to drive a motor vehicle but Burg (1967)[3] measured five parameters of vision in 17,500 Californian drivers and compared these with their three-year accident histories. The survey reviewed 5,200 accidents: drivers had to estimate their mileage and accident rates per 100,000 miles travelled were calculated. The study showed only a weak, although statistically significant, correlation between the scores on the five tests of vision and drivers' accident rates. Dynamic visual acuity, the ability to follow a series of rapidly moving targets on a screen, proved to be the most significant accident predictor, but this, even then was only a poor predictor. Later, Burg's computer tapes were re-analysed by Hills and Burg (1977)[4] at the British Transport Research Laboratory in relation to the age of drivers and they were unable to show a relationship between reduced performance on the five tests and above average accident rates below the age of 54 years. There was a weak statistical relationship for visual acuity (Snellen Test) and also for dynamic visual acuity in drivers over 54 years. There was no accident correlation in persons with reduced total visual fields.

Epilepsy presents a particular problem in that the sudden nature of incapacitation is reflected in the relatively high incidence of epilepsy factor accidents against other medical factor accidents. The part played by epilepsy has been comprehensively reviewed by the report `Epilepsy

PREVALENCE OF MEDICAL FACTORS IN ROAD TRAFFIC ACCIDENTS

and Driver Licence Regulations' published by the International Bureau for Epilepsy and the International League Against Epilepsy[5] – the minority of people with epilepsy who drive seem to have an about average accident rate but with greater injury and fatality involvement.[6] It has to be seen in the context of a threefold accident risk over average for young male drivers. Most countries now allow people with epilepsy to drive passenger cars and motorcycles if they have been free from seizures for a reasonable period, but Germany, Japan and India still apply a ban.

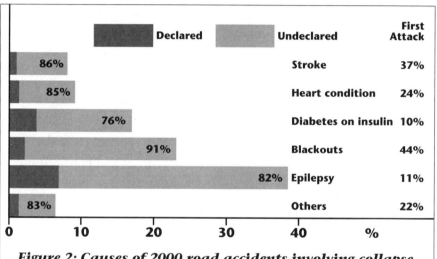

Figure 2: Causes of 2000 road accidents involving collapse at wheel, based on reports by the police to the DVLC

Coronary heart disease is very prevalent in the British population and patient risk factor analysis is frequently adopted. Interestingly, about a quarter of heart attacks, occurring whilst driving and leading to a road traffic accident, are first attack cases,[7] but overall comprise only ten per cent of medical factor road traffic accidents.

Alcohol is the most important human factor in road traffic accidents. Over the last ten or so years the number of driver fatalities where alcohol was found in the body fluids over the legal limit of blood/alcohol concentration of 0.08 per cent has decreased from one in three to now approximately one in five drivers. Simpson and Mayhew 1992 (personal communication) estimate that approximately one per cent of the driving population with blood alcohol concentrations of 0.15% and above are over 200 times more likely to be involved in a fatal crash than average non-drinking drivers.

The *drugs* found in the body fluids of 1,273 people killed in British road accidents between 1985 and 1988 were quantitatively and qualitatively assessed. Cannabis was present in 2.8 per cent, but urinalysis of out-patient attenders at a London hospital at about the same time showed cannabinoids in over 20 per cent of patients. The only psycho-active drugs that appeared to be over-represented in this fatality study were the anti-convulsants which appeared to be four times in excess on the basis of the British population of people with epilepsy and the estimated number of drivers with epilepsy. It can probably be assumed that it was not the anti-convulsants that were associated with the fatalities but rather the underlying epilepsy.

Obstructive sleep apnoea as a cause of excessive awake-time sleepiness and driving accidents has recently come to prominence following publication of the 1993 Royal College of Physician's of London Working Party report.[8] Findlay[9] reviewed the accident rates of 29 patients with obstructive sleep apnoea who were drivers registered in the state of Virginia. He showed that they had 2.6 times the average accident rate for drivers in the state, but when the 29 were age and sex matched against 35 people who did not have sleep apnoea their accident rate was seven times that of the control group. Stradling[10] has reviewed over 1,000 Oxfordshire middle-aged men and found a prevalence rate of obstructive sleep apnoea of one per cent.

PREVALENCE OF MEDICAL FACTORS
IN ROAD TRAFFIC ACCIDENTS

Medical and other factors in Road Accidents

Research on overall aspects of medical fitness causing road traffic accidents in the UK was carried out in 1968 by Grattan and Jeffcoate.[11] They reviewed 9,930 injury accidents and found that 15 were caused by episodes of some kind of acute illness. Among these were three cases of epilepsy (0.3% of the total). The injuries due to acute illness episodes tended to be more severe than usual, eight being serious and seven minor in nature. Overall they estimated that 1.5:1000 RTAs had acute medical factor involvement but this became 1:250 in serious injury RTAs. Other EEC countries and the USA have confirmed a similar accident rate, validating the WHO statement that "all forms of sudden illness combined are probably responsible for about one accident per thousand involving injury" (WHO 1966).[12] The Department of Transport annually publishes a review `Road Accident Statistics Great Britain, The Casualty Report'. This highlights the problem of poly-causal accidents and draws attention to the much more serious consequences of accidents involving buses and large goods vehicles compared with cars and motorcycles. The former have three to five times the fatality rate for road users compared with those involving light vehicles. The probable explanation is that the larger vehicles with concomitant higher energy are involved in multiple vehicle pile-ups. But driver incapacitation, if it is going to happen, is more likely to occur at the wheel in a vocational driver because of the longer hours spent driving.

Road Accident Fatality Rates

Britain has one of the lowest fatality rates for RTAs per 100 million vehicle kilometres travelled apart the US (Figure 3 overleaf). Japan has shown the most dramatic improvement. Britain remains better than Australia in spite of their targeted random breath testing programme.

PREVALENCE OF MEDICAL FACTORS
IN ROAD TRAFFIC ACCIDENTS

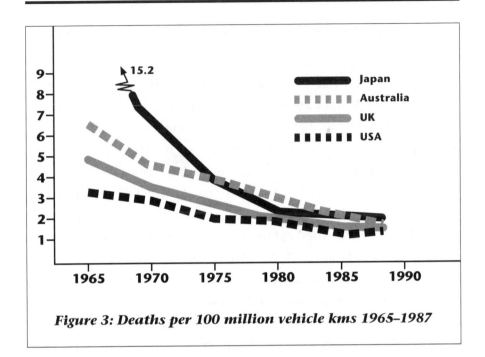

Figure 3: Deaths per 100 million vehicle kms 1965–1987

Age and Accidents

Figure 4 shows British driver accident frequency relating to age by computer modelling. Research suggests that driving experience is more important than age. The elderly tend to drive progressively less each year so that accident involvement becomes progressively less with age. Elderly drivers have a higher propensity to accidents joining major roads and turning right. They tend to avoid night driving due to their sensitivity to glare and try to confine their driving to familiar routes. An 18 year old driver has over 3 times the accident involvement per year than a 70 year old driver.

Figure 4 illustrates the sensitivity of accident liability to driving experience by showing how predicted accident frequency would change with driving experience.

PREVALENCE OF MEDICAL FACTORS IN ROAD TRAFFIC ACCIDENTS

Group II driving

UK legislation imposes higher (Group II) medical standards for larger vehicle drivers (See Chapter 2, Part I). These higher standards are justified because professional drivers spend substantially longer at the wheel than do private motorists, so that the risk of sudden illness occurring whilst actually driving is greater. Heavy vehicles including larger buses and lorries, due to their size and weight have a greater fatality rate per mile travelled than do cars. For buses the fatality rate is four times, per mile travelled than for cars and for Large Goods Vehicles, it is three times that for cars. Sudden collapse at the wheel in bus drivers who approach queues of people, often many times per working shift can have very serious consequences. Some goods vehicles carry dangerous cargoes and spillage of these can lead to dire consequences in the event of an accident. Furthermore it is not easy for a professional driver to stop driving if he is feeling unwell due to schedules that have to be maintained. Taxi, emergency ambulance and emergency police drivers should be required to meet Group II standards, although the EU directives do not specifically include these classes of vehicles.

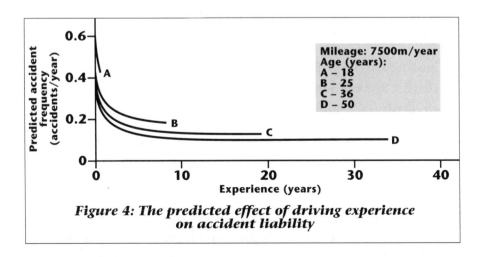

Figure 4: The predicted effect of driving experience on accident liability

PREVALENCE OF MEDICAL FACTORS IN ROAD TRAFFIC ACCIDENTS

Age is an important risk factor in those with a previous history of symptomatic coronary heart and cerebrovascular disease. Evidence suggests that persons who develop severe or even fatal attacks may have sufficient warning to slow down or even stop the vehicle before losing consciousness. But, not infrequently, no warning occurs or a warning symptom is misinterpreted or ignored by the driver and this may result in severe injury or death to other drivers or pedestrians. It is therefore advisable to recommend that Group II driving should be discontinued in patients with a history of symptomatic cerebrovascular and coronary heart disease, at least by the age of 65 years. Many of course voluntarily retire before that age.

REFERENCES

1. Sabey B E, Staughton G C. Interacting Roles of Road Environment, Vehicle and Road User Accidents. Paper presented at 5th International Conference of the International Association of Accident and Traffic Medicine – London, September 1975.

2. Treat J R, Tumbas N S, McDonald ST et al. Trilevel Study of Cause of Traffic Accidents. Report No. DOT–HS–034–3–5–35–77 (TAC). Indiana University, March 1988.

3. Burg A (1967). The Relationship between Vision Test Scores and Driving Record: General Findings. Report No. 67–24. Los Angeles: University of California, Department of Engineering.

4. Hills RL and Burg A (1977). A Reanalysis of California Driver Vision Data: General Findings. Research report LR 768 Transport and Road Research Laboratory, Crowthorne, England.

5. Epilepsy and Driving Licence Regulations. Report by the International Bureau for Epilepsy and International League Against

Epilepsy, September 1992, PO Box 21, 210 AA Heemsteede, The Netherlands.

6. University Department of Neurosurgical Science at Liverpool report unpublished at time of going to press

7. Taylor J. Medical Fitness to Drive. In: Harrington J M edited Recent Advances in Occupational Health. Edinburgh: Churchill Livingstone 1987: 103.

8. Sleep Apnoea and Related Conditions (Oct. 1993). The Royal college of Physicians, London.

9. Findlay L J, Unverza G T M E, Suratt P M. Automobile Accidents Involving Patients with Obstructive Sleep Apnoea. Am Rev. Respir Dis. August 1988 138 (2) P337–40.

10. Stradling JR, Crosby JH. Predictors and Prevalence of Obstructive Sleep Apnoea and Snoring in 1,001 Middle Aged Men. Thorax 1991: 46: 85–90.

11. Grattan E and Jeffcoate GO (1968). Medical Factors and Road Accidents. British Medical Journal, 1, 75.

12. World Health Organisation (1966). Report of Inter-Regional Seminar on Epidemiology Control and Prevention of Road Traffic Accidents/WHO/Accid. Prev. 66.6.

13. Transport Research paper 315 Transport Research Laboratory, Crowthorne, Berks.

2

PART 1:

LEGAL PROVISIONS RELATING TO THE STANDARDS OF MEDICAL FITNESS REQUIRED FOR BRITISH LICENCE HOLDERS AND APPLICANTS

1. The licensing authority

The Secretary of State for Transport has the responsibility for granting driving licences, and his duties are discharged by the DVLA in Swansea. A team of doctors provide the medical advice on which the Secretary of State decides whether or not an applicant for, or holder of, a licence is fit to drive.

2. Applications for licences

The application for a licence is made on form D1 obtainable from a Post Office. An application for a bus or lorry licence – (Group II) – has to include a medical report form D4 also obtainable from Post Offices. The address in regard to medical enquiries is The Driving and Vehicle Licensing Centre, DVLA, Swansea SA99 1TU. Telephone enquiries on medical aspects for fitness to drive should be made on 01792 783686. A leaflet explaining the medical and other aspects of driving licensing (D100) is also obtainable from Post Offices.

3. The duty of applicant

When applying for a licence, an applicant must declare whether he is or has suffered at any time from any relevant or prospective disability.

PART 1:
LEGAL PROVISIONS

4. Disabilities

Relevant disabilities for driving licence purposes are categorised as follows:

i) Specific disabilities which are prescribed by regulations made under the Act, such as epilepsy, and;

ii) Any disability which is likely to cause the driving of a vehicle to be a source of danger on the roads.

iii) Relevant limb disabilities which are static such as traumatic loss of a limb.

Prospective disabilities are those disabilities, which, although at the time of the application are not relevant disabilities, are likely to become such in the course of time.

Where an applicant is found to be suffering from a relevant disability in (i) or (ii) above, the Secretary of State must refuse the grant of a licence (subject to some exceptions).

In the case of static limb disabilities (iii) above, the arbiter is a driving test.

5. Provision of information

If a licence holder becomes aware that he is suffering from a disability (either prospective or relevant) which has not been previously disclosed, he must notify the Secretary of State of the nature and extent of the disability.

The Secretary of State also has the power to require a person to give consent to his doctors and specialists to provide medical reports and also to attend a doctor for a medical examination to determine if he is fit to drive. Refusal to do so can be sufficient grounds to permit the Secretary of State to refuse an application or revoke a licence.

PART 1:
LEGAL PROVISIONS

6. Prescribed disabilities

The following are prescribed disabilities for the purposes of the 1988 Act:

a) epilepsy;

b) severe mental handicap;

c) liability to sudden attacks of disabling giddiness or fainting, other than such attacks falling within paragraph (d);

d) liability to sudden attacks of disabling giddiness or fainting which are caused by any disorder or defect of the heart as a result of which the applicant for the licence or, as the case may be, the holder of the licence has a device implanted in his body, being a device which, by operating on the heart so as to regulate its action, is designed to correct the disorder or defect; and

e) inability to read in good daylight (with the aid of glasses or contact lenses if worn) a registration mark fixed to a motor vehicle and containing letters and figures 79.4 millimetres high at a distance of:

i) 20.5 metres, in any case except that mentioned below; or

ii) 12.3 metres, in the case of an applicant for a licence authorising the driver of vehicles of a class included in category K only.

7. Additional disabilities of Group II applicants

In addition to the disabilities listed above, the following are also disabilities for LGV/PCV applicants and licence holders:

a) liability to epileptic seizures;

b) abnormal sight in one or both eyes where:

PART 1:
LEGAL PROVISIONS

i) *in the case of a person who held an existing licence on 1st January 1983 and who holds such a licence on 1st April 1991, the visual acuity is worse than 6/12 with the better eye and worse than 6/36 with the other eye and, if corrective lenses are worn, the uncorrected acuity in each eye is worse than 3/60, or*

ii) *in a case of a person not falling within paragraph (1)(b)(i) above who held a licence or an existing licence on 1st March 1992, the visual acuity is worse than 6/9 in the better eye and worse than 6/12 in the other eye and, if corrective lenses are worn, the uncorrected acuity in each eye is worse than 3/60, or*

iii) *in any other case, the visual acuity is worse than 6/9 in the better eye or worse than 6/12 in the other eye or, if corrective lenses have to be worn to ensure that the visual acuity in one eye or both eyes is no worse than 6/9 in the better eye and 6/12 in the other eye, the uncorrected acuity in each eye is worse than 3/60;*

c) sight in only one eye unless:

i) *in the case of a person who held an existing licence on 1st January 1983 and who holds such a licence on 1st April 1991 the traffic commissioner in whose area he resides or the traffic commissioner who granted the last-mentioned licence knew of the disability before 1st January 1991 and the visual acuity in that eye is no worse than 6/12, or*

ii) *in the case of a person who did not hold an existing licence on 1st January 1983 but who holds an existing licence on 1st April 1991 the traffic commissioner in whose area he resides or the traffic commissioner who granted the last-mentioned licence knew of the disability before 1st January 1991 and the visual acuity in that eye is no worse than 6/9;*

PART 1:
LEGAL PROVISIONS

With effect from 1st July 1996 all new applicants and those same applicants on renewal:

a) *"must have a visual acuity, with corrective lenses if necessary, of at least 0.8 in the better eye and at least 0.5 in the worse eye" – this corresponds to 6/9 and 6/12 respectively on the Snellen scale;*

b) *if corrective lenses are used, "the uncorrected acuity in each eye must reach 0.05" – equivalent to 3/60 on the Snellen scale;*

c) *must have a normal field of vision in both eyes;*

d) *must not be suffering from diplopia (double vision).*

These will be incorporated in UK legislation effective from the above date.

9. Diabetes subject to insulin treatment

Unless the person in question held, on 1st April 1991, an existing licence and the traffic commissioner in whose area he resides or the traffic commissioner who granted the licence knew of the disability before 1st January 1991.

10. Loss of a limb

Applicants for licences suffering from a Static Limb Disability have an automatic right in Great Britain to a provisional driving licence for the purpose of taking a driving test to prove their ability to drive. Normally provisional licences run until the applicants 70th birthday, except in

PART 1:
LEGAL PROVISIONS

the case of motorcycle entitlement which only runs for 2 years and cannot be renewed until a year has elapsed unless a test has been passed.

11. Duration of licences

The motorcar driving licence currently covers light goods vehicles and minibuses and normally runs until the age of 70, but persons with medical conditions likely to be progressive, or intermittent may, at the discretion of the licensing authority have their licences restricted to one, two or three years. After the age of 70 these licences are renewable, normally on a 3 yearly basis on payment of a fee. Medically restricted short period licences are not charged a fee. Large goods vehicles currently are those with a laden weight of, or in excess of, 7.5 tonnes. From the 1st July 1996 when the second EU Driver Licensing Directive comes into force, new light goods and minibus drivers, will be required to meet Group II standards to drive vehicles of 3.5 metric tonnes laden weight or more or passenger carrying vehicles having nine seats or more, but will not be required for vehicles operated by certain voluntary groups. Emergency, ambulances, police and firemen as well as taxi drivers are not specifically singled out in driver licensing legislation but taxi drivers are licensed by local authorities under local government legislation. The Medical Commission on Accident Prevention recommends that Group II standards should be applicable to drivers of these vehicles. Group II licences normally expire after the forty-fifth birthday and are renewable every 5 years up to the age of 65 and annually thereafter. Each application has to include a medical report on from D4 completed by a registered medical practitioner, most commonly the general practitioner. If company doctors are not familiar with an applicant's medical history they are advised to consult the patient's General Practitioner.

PART 1:
LEGAL PROVISIONS

12. Appeal

Where a driving licence is refused or revoked on medical grounds or restricted in period of duration, there is a right of appeal to a Magistrates' Court in England and Wales or to a Sheriffs Court in Scotland.

13. New UK Legislation

New UK legislation will be introduced prior to the coming into force of the EU Driving Licence Directive on 1 July 1996. Most of the EU directive medical standards have already been incorporated in UK law but more specific regulations relating to not issuing or renewing driving licences to persons with:

i)   serious arrhythmias

ii)   severe mental disorders

iii) severe behavioural problems

iv)   alcohol dependency

v)   inability to refrain from drinking and driving

vi)   drug abuse and dependency

vii) psychotropic medicines taken in quantities likely to impair fitness to drive safely

viii) the visual standards in para 7 above for Group II in bold print.

will be prescribed and failure to meet these absolute standards will be a relevant disability.

2

PART 2:
MEDICO-LEGAL CONSIDERATIONS

Principal Authors: Dr Peter Schutte[¥] and Dr John Barker*

1. Doctors' Liability in Certifying Fitness to Drive

The responsibility for determining the fitness to drive of an individual
rests with the DVLA. All licence holders have a responsibility to inform
the DVLA if they develop a medical condition or if an existing one
worsens which may affect their fitness to drive. Doctors may be asked
to provide a report for the DVLA, but this will not include an opinion
on the patient's fitness to drive.

The DVLA has the statutory responsibility for certifying individuals as
fit to drive Group II. Doctors are required to undertake no more than
the examination and completion of form D4. The form does not ask
for an opinion on fitness to drive.

The responsibility for licensing taxi and hire car drivers, to comply with
local requirements, rests with the local traffic authority. Taxis and hire
cars are not PCVs under the provisions of the Passenger Vehicles Act
1981, and doctors may be asked to certify fitness to drive for the local
authority. Doctors may also be asked by their patients to provide a
certificate of fitness to drive for an insurance company. These fall
outside the NHS and may attract a fee.

Doctors providing certificates for local authorities and insurance
companies, where they know of no medical condition which would
render the patient unfit to drive, should be aware of a potential liability.

¥   *Medical Defence Union.*
*   *Medical Protection Society.*

PART 2:
MEDICO-LEGAL CONSIDERATIONS

Third party motor insurance damages are compulsorily payable by Insurers who can reclaim costs from others who are negligent. A doctor certifying a person as fit, without due care and skill, or contrary to national guidelines, could be found to be negligent and be held liable for the costs incurred by the motor insurer.

Doctors facing allegations of this nature may look to their defence organisations in the usual way to provide discretionary indemnity.

Confidentiality

All doctors owe their patients a duty of confidentiality. This duty may be enforced by the General Medical Council (GMC). Difficulties may arise when a doctor feels the need to breach confidentiality in the public interest and this may occur particularly with regard to fitness to drive.

The GMC recognises that on rare occasions a doctor may breach confidentiality in the public interest where failure to do so may place the patient or some other person at risk of serious harm or death. In the first instance, the doctor should advise the patient to inform the DVLA of any condition, or deterioration in an existing condition, which may affect the patient's fitness to drive. However, it may come to the doctor's attention that the patient may have failed to do so or may continue to drive contrary to the doctor's advice, pending a determination by the DVLA.

The patient should be challenged, and where appropriate, advised that the doctor will inform the DVLA directly. Only in exceptional circumstances will the doctor inform the DVLA without first warning the patient and/or on the basis that the source of the information will not be revealed by the DVLA to the patient.

The doctor might become aware that a patient's licence has been

PART 2:
MEDICO-LEGAL CONSIDERATIONS

revoked by the DVLA, but that he continues to drive. It may then be appropriate for the doctor to inform the local police.

Doctors should only breach confidentiality in good faith and after careful thought. Members of a defence organisation are recommended to discuss such cases with a medico-legal adviser in advance.

Notwithstanding the above, when a patient has a serious medical condition likely to make them a danger to themselves and others if they drive, the doctor should confidentially inform a DVLA Medical Adviser without delay (telephone number 01792 783686) where the condition of the patient is such that they are unable or unlikely to be able to notify DVLA (e.g. demented or psychotic patients).

3

THE OLDER DRIVER

Principal Author: John Taylor*

Morbidity increases with age and medical factors adverse to safe driving may be multiple and synergistic. Basically, however, achieving medical fitness depends on meeting the fitness standards of the individual chapters in this book. There is no age bar to the holding of a driving licence. Changes with age vary from one person to another, with no necessary correspondence between biological age and age in years.

Accident Involvement

Older drivers tend to drive less miles per year than their younger counter-parts. The highest accident rate per mile travelled involved group is females aged over 74. This may be because many married women in single car families let their husbands do most of the driving, but have to return to driving in their latter years due to widowhood or disablement of their husband. Accident involvement progressively falls from very high levels in drivers under age 25 but begins to increase modestly from age 65. However, when looking at fatal accidents, the older driver is at greater risk of being killed due to the fragility of the aged body.

Figure 1 shows a rapidly increasing trend in the population of drivers over the age of 65. In spite of this dramatically increasing trend, figure 2b shows a fall in the percentage of male car driver casualties between 1979 and 1989 (from 10% of all casualties to 6%) in the age group 60–69. Male driver casualties between 70 and 79 have also shown a lesser reduction but age 80+ male drivers have shown a modest percentage increase which probably accords with the fragility of the older body. In spite of the increasing percentage of women driving licence holders over 65, their

*   *Chairman Transport Committee, Medical Commission on Accident Prevention.*

casualty involvement continues unchanged at about 1.5% of total road traffic accident casualties. But again, there is a modest increase in the percentage of female casualty drivers over the age of 80.

Figure 1: Percentage of Age Group holding a Car Driving Licence						
	1965		**1985**		**Increase 1985/1965**	
Age Group	Male %	Fem. %	Male %	Fem. %	Male %	Fem. %
17–59	55	12	71	47	29	290
60–64	41	6	74	28	80	366
65+	19	2	57	14	200	600

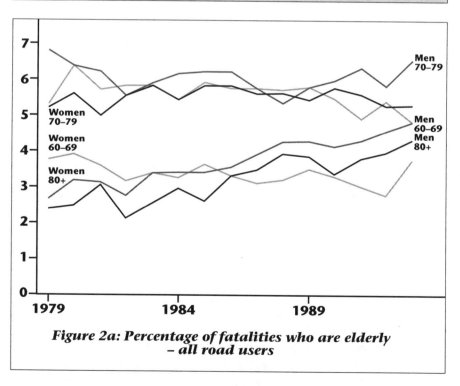

Figure 2a: Percentage of fatalities who are elderly – all road users

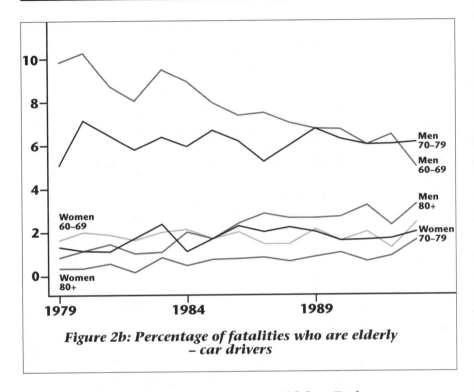

*Figure 2b: Percentage of fatalities who are elderly
– car drivers*

Choosing a Car as an Older Driver

Generally, it is unwise to change from a manual to automatic over the age of 70 unless it is due to limb disabilities. It is sensible, however, to make this change in the 50s so as to get well used to it. Automatic transmission is much easier to adapt to disabled controls and 3/4 of strokes occur over the age of 65. Power steering is of advantage to the older driver as it facilitates parking. Tinted windows should be avoided as they do not reduce glare but do reduce visual acuity.

Vision and the Older Driver

Vision may start to fade with age. Cataracts may begin to develop from the age of 40. Moderate degrees of lens opacity cause glare sensitivity so that driving against on-coming headlights at night becomes particularly painful and dangerous. It is prudent for the older driver so afflicted to plan journeys and avoid night driving on unlit roads where possible. The Road Traffic Act visual acuity requirement is to read a number plate fixed to a vehicle in good daylight with glasses or contact lenses if worn, at 67 feet (20.5 metres). This is an absolute requirement in law – see Vision chapter – and to drive when unable to meet this standard is a criminal offence. The Number Plate Test can be readily self-applied at the roadside by measuring up a length of string and tying it to the number plate. Regular self testing is recommended and the cure for failure may be cataract surgery. Tinted lenses and antiglare spectacles reduce night vision rather than improve it and should be avoided when driving at night. Because glaucoma can insidiously develop and if undetected and untreated can lead to permanent visual field damage, it is sensible for the elderly to have a professional eye test at least every 2 years.

Sleepiness, Alcohol and Medicines and the Older Driver

Sleepiness may become a problem for the older driver. Even the smallest amounts of alcohol can provoke falling asleep at the wheel, which in law is no defence against a charge of dangerous driving. Prescribed medicines should be those that do not induce somnolence. Motorway hard shoulders are no place to rest if fatigued. 14% of fatalities on motorways occur on the hard shoulder. In the absence of a decent night's sleep, it is wise not to undertake prolonged driving the following day. However, if somnolence happens at the wheel on the motorway, it is essential to leave at the first opportunity. Many junctions have laybys and some have service areas nearby. Sleepiness can only be cured by sleep. Coffee and tea can help but alcohol makes somnolence much worse.

THE OLDER DRIVER

Road Accident Situations

Joining major roads and turning right particularly feature in accidents involving older drivers. Older drivers should never be panicked into taking a risk in these circumstances, they should relax and take their time and not be egged on by an impatient following driver.

Taking Rear and Lateral Observation

This can be difficult when the spinal joints become stiff. American work suggests that regular spinal exercises, twisting one's head on neck and trunk can promote looser spinal joints and improve rear observation when driving. That apart, it is wise to have adequate and well-placed mirrors. A particularly difficulty is joining motorways from acute angled feeder roads. One trick is to lean forward and look into the door mirror as this gives a wider field of view. Wing mirrors give a better rear view than door mirrors. The use of "Blind Spot" wedge shaped supplementary rear view mirrors is strongly recommended. Glasses with thick frames and side pieces should be avoided.

Giving up Driving

Giving up driving is not easy for the older driver. Economics show that its cheaper travel by public transport and taxis etc. if annual mileage is below 4,000. Where there is doubt about ability to safely drive due to age rather than medical conditions, one solution is a trial driving lesson by a driving school instructor to get a dispassionate view. Sometimes a few brush-up lessons can restore confidence and safe driving. This is particularly applicable to those who have not driven for many years and who have to return to driving in their later years.

4

CARDIOVASCULAR DISEASE

Principal Author: Dr Michael Petch MD FRCP FACC*

Introduction

Cardiovascular disease is very common and accounts for about one half of all deaths in the United Kingdom.[1] Approximately one quarter of all deaths are due to coronary heart disease.[1] Death is commonly sudden. Yet heart disease is a rare cause of road traffic accidents. When sudden death is averted by out of hospital resuscitation the usual early finding is ventricular fibrillation.[2] Experience in coronary care units and elsewhere suggests that the heart rhythm degenerates rapidly into this lethal arrhythmia. Death may be sudden in epidemiological terms but is not instantaneous. Thus a driver may have a brief moment in which to pull into the side of the road and stop. This accords with published evidence,[3,4] e.g. "a driver was commonly found dead at the wheel of his vehicle beside the road, with the engine still running".[4]

Cardiovascular collapse can nevertheless be instantaneous, the Stokes-Adams attack due to heart block being a classic example. The abrupt loss of consciousness due to a cardiac arrhythmia is the most feared hazard for the middle-aged driver, but other less sinister disorders such as the development of cardiac pain or the onset of a usually benign arrhythmia, e.g. atrial fibrillation, may be sufficient to impair a driver's attention and lead to an accident. Regulations and guidelines for drivers must therefore take into account not only published data on the natural history of cardiovascular disease, which tend to deal with major events such as death and heart attack, but also the wealth of clinical experience that has accumulated since the publication of previous

---

*   *Consultant Cardiologist, Papworth Hospital, Cambridge CB38RE.*

31

editions of this booklet. In general this has led to a relaxation and simplification of the previous guidelines. For example, prosthetic heart valves and cardiac pacemakers are now known to be reliable; re-stenosis following coronary angioplasty is usually gradual and causes recurrent angina, not myocardial infarction; electrophysiological testing has transformed our understanding of arrhythmias; exercise testing has largely supplanted coronary angiography in the risk assessment of individuals with coronary heart disease.

The principles underlying the assessment of drivers with cardiovascular disease have to recognise that cardiovascular disorders are a rare cause of accidents (see Chapter 1). Striking a balance between the liberty of the individual driver and the risk that a particular driver with heart disease presents to other road users, is always going to be imperfect and to some extent frustrated by the fact that a significant minority of cardiac events at the wheel will occur in drivers who have no previous evidence of cardiovascular disease. Nevertheless, certain drivers at certain times in their lives are at relatively high risk of cardiovascular collapse, e.g. those with recent myocardial infarction or unstable angina.

A clinical and non invasive approach to assessment has been preferred with it's emphasis on the history, physical examination and cardiography although there are specific instances where other technical measurements are essential e.g. the diameter of an aortic aneurysm. The arbiter is the Secretary of State as licensing authority who delegates these matters to his medical advisers based at DVLA. They can seek additional advice from a panel of experts – The Honorary Medical Advisory Panel to the Secretary of State on Driving and Disorders of the Heart.

Three quarters of people who collapse at the wheel on account of heart attacks have a previous history of heart disease.[5] The argument that the greatest risk stems from the multitude of drivers who have never previously experienced any cardiac condition is not correct. The major risk of sudden incapacity is soon after the event. The legal test that has to be applied by DVLA in determining unfitness of any drivers is Section 92 of the 1988 Road Traffic Act. This precludes the grant of any driving licence, where the applicant is suffering from a disability which is "likely to cause the driving of a motor vehicle by him in pursuance of a licence to be a source of danger to the Public". "Likely" has been clarified in Case law as "something more than a bare possibility but less than probable".[6] DVLA has to take immediate action in revoking the driving licence if, for example, a Group II driver notifies DVLA within three months of the cardiac episode. Medical practitioners also have a duty of care to advise their patients accordingly.

Practitioners should be reminded that Group I (ordinary) drivers do not need to notify DVLA unless there is continuing disability from a cardiovascular cause, however all Group II (vocational) drivers must notify DVLA immediately after an event.

Commentary on guidelines

The guidelines are appended to this chapter in italics. In general the reasoning behind them will be apparent to most readers. For ordinary drivers (group one entitlement) the very simple recommendation is to stop driving for one month after a cardiac event and report any subsequent continuing disability to the DVLA. Arrhythmias which may render a driver liable to recurrent attacks of impaired consciousness are an absolute bar to the holding of any class of driving licence.

The guidelines undergo change as new treatments are introduced. At the time of writing this applies particularly to the management of cardiac arrhythmias. The implantable cardioverter defibrillator (ICD)

CARDIOVASCULAR DISEASE

is a relatively new form of treatment for patients with malignant ventricular arrhythmias. In principle the device recognises such an arrhythmia and charges up over a period of about 20 seconds before delivering a shock. The arrhythmia or the shock itself may be sufficient to distract a driver and on occasions the devices may be falsely triggered by benign arrhythmia such as atrial fibrillation. Experience with these devices, as compared with for example conventional pacemakers and prosthetic heart valves is very limited but will accumulate as time goes on. At the time of going to press driving is not permitted but this recommendation is under review.

The cardiovascular diseases that affect vocational drivers (Group II entitlement) nearly always involve specialist cardiological or hospital management, e.g. coronary heart disease, heart valve replacement, congenital heart disease, cardiomyopathy, and pacemakers; most vocational drivers with these conditions will already have had access to expert advice and the relevant investigations notably exercise testing.

Exercise testing is a valuable prognostic tool in evaluating Group II drivers with a past history of coronary heart disease who meet all the other criteria of medical fitness. The current recommendation demands completion of three stages of the Bruce protocol (equivalent to ten mets) safely. The word safely is important as it is clearly essential that the supervisor should terminate the test if it is deemed unsafe to continue. The result is also deemed to be unacceptable if there is evidence of myocardial ischaemia e.g. angina, cardiac dyspnoea, fall in BP, sustained ventricular tachycardia or pathological ST segment shift. If symptoms attributable to angina or peripheral vascular disease limit completion of the investigation, the test is also deemed unacceptable. Interpretation of ST shift as "pathological" needs to take cognisance of the heart rate and/or workload, as well as any pre-existing ST segment abnormality (as commonly occurs, for example after coronary artery

Cardiovascular Disease

bypass surgery, or in the case of patients taking digitalis glycosides). To be acceptable, exercise testing must be performed off cardio-active medication, especially nitrates which can prevent angina and enhance an individual's performance so that his true limitation and prognosis is concealed. The exercise standard adopted is justified by published evidence e.g. Weiner et al (1984)7 who studied 4,083 medically treated patients with symptomatic coronary heart disease. They reviewed mortality at 4 years and found the ST segment response and duration of exercise proved the most important exercise test variables. They identified an extremely low risk group (32%) with an annual mortality of 1% or less, who could exercise into Stage III or greater of the Bruce protocol with less than 1mm ST segment depression on the ECG. In contrast, a high risk group (12%) comprised those who could only exercise into Stage I Bruce and who had ST depression of at least 1mm with an annual mortality of 5% or more. These authors also confirmed the overriding prognostic importance of left ventricular function and the poor survival of patients with heart failure.

The clinical and exercise test variables enable the risk of a cardiac event to be assessed in a population. But an individual patient may not conform hence many cardiologists will often recommend angiography. Exercise testing and Angiography provide equally valuable but rather different information about the heart. The former is physiological, the latter mainly anatomical. Both assist in assessing the risk of a cardiovascular event and both have to be taken into consideration.

References

1. Coronary Heart disease Statistics British Heart Foundation 1994.

2. Greene H.L.(1990) Sudden Arrhythmic Cardiac Death Mechanisms Resuscitation and Classification – The Seattle Perspective. AM. Journal of Card. Vol. 65 4B–12B.

CARDIOVASCULAR DISEASE

3. Hossack D.W.(1980) Medical Catastrophes at the Wheel. Med. J. Of Australia, 1:327–328

4. Christian MS, (1988) Incidence and Implications of Natural death of Road Users. British Medical Journal, Vol. 297.

5. Taylor J.F.(1989). Driving and Epilepsy. New draft EU directive for a Common Community driving licence. Royal Society of Medicine London, International Congress and Symposium Series No.152 P270–271.

6. Benigton V. Peter. Regina v Swaffham Justices Ex parte Peter. Before Mr Justice Woolf Judgement delivered 7. Feb 1984.

7. Weiner, D.A., Ryan, T.J., McCabe, C.H. et al.(1984): Prognostic importance of a clinical profile and exercise test in medically treated patients with coronary artery disease. J.Am. Coll. Cardiol. 3:772.

CARDIOVASCULAR DISEASE

The applicant or licence holder must notify DVLA unless stated otherwise in the text.

CARDIOVASCULAR DISORDERS	GROUP I ENTITLEMENT	GROUP II ENTITLEMENT
ANGINA	If angina occurs at wheel driving must cease and will not be permitted until satisfactory control of symptoms is achieved. Till 70 retained.	Recommended permanent refusal or revocation if symptoms are continuing – or even if they are controlled on medication.
HEART FAILURE	Driving may be permitted when satisfactory control of symptoms is achieved. Till 70 retained.	Recommended permanent refusal or revocation whether or not maintained symptom free by the use of medication.
MYOCARDIAL INFARCTION, CORONARY ARTERY BY-PASS GRAFT ANY EPISODE OF UNSTABLE ANGINA	At least one month off driving after the event is recommended. If satisfactory recovery, driving may restart. Till 70 retained. DVLA need not be notified provided there are no disqualifying conditions in other sections.	Driving to cease for 3 months – return to driving will be permitted when the person is symptom free (see angina/heart failure section etc.), there are no other disqualifying conditions and the person is able to complete the exercise test to the required standard. (See the end of this section for the required standard).
CORONARY ANGIOPLASTY		
	At least 1 week off driving after the event is recommended. If satisfactory recovery, driving may restart. Till 70 retained. DVLA need not be notified provided there are no other disqualifying conditions.	CORONARY ANGIOGRAM IS NOT REQUIRED FOR LICENSING PURPOSES

CARDIOVASCULAR DISEASE

CARDIOVASCULAR DISORDERS	GROUP I ENTITLEMENT	GROUP II ENTITLEMENT
PERIPHERAL VASCULAR DISEASE	DVLA need not be notified, driving may continue. Till 70 retained.	Refusal/Revocation if there is clinical evidence of associated ischaemic heart disease.
AORTIC ANEURYSM with a diameter greater than 5 cm.		Driving will be only permitted after satisfactory repair – provided there is no clinical evidence of cardiac ischaemia.
Dissection of the Aorta.	Driving will be permitted on recovery and the Till 70 licence retained.	Permanent Refusal/Revocation.
ARRHYTHMIA (including any significant disturbance of cardiac rhythm, i.e. bradycardia due to atrioventricular block (including congenital heart block) or sinus node disease; or a supraventricular (including atrial flutter and fibrillation), junctional or ventricular tachyarrhythmia.	Driving must cease with an arrhythmia which may distract the driver's attention or render him/her liable to sudden impairment of cerebral function. Driving will be permitted when satisfactory control of symptoms is achieved. Short period licence subject to regular medical review for patients with history of idiopathic ventricular tachyarrhythmia. Till 70 retained (ventricular tachyarrhythmia excepted) provided there are no other disqualifying conditions.	Recommended refusal or revocation if persistent or recurrent arrhythmia or conduction defect within the past 5 years and has caused within the past 2 years or is likely to cause sudden impairment of consciousness or distracts the driver's attention. If the arrhythmia does not cause such symptoms, may be licensed if there is no significant structural cardiac abnormality, i.e. no documented significant echocardiographic abnormality is present, and exercise testing can be completed as per national guidelines. In exercise testing for arrhythmias medication need not be discontinued before test is undertaken.

CARDIOVASCULAR DISORDERS	GROUP I ENTITLEMENT	GROUP II ENTITLEMENT
ARRHYTHMIA (continued)		Medication prescribed to control or prevent the arrhythmia is not a bar, provided it does not cause symptoms likely to impair driver's performance (see Drug Treatment).
NB: Transient Arrhythmias occurring within the acute phase of a coronary event or heart surgery normally will not debar and the recommendations for arrhythmia for Group I and 2 entitlement therefore do not apply to events in the acute phase.		Where rhythm disturbance is treated by aberrant pathway ablation relicensing may occur 3 months after procedure provided: 1) no recurrence 2) no anti-arrhythmic medication required and no other disbarring aspect/condition is present.
PACEMAKER INSERTION	Driving must cease for 1 month. Provided insertion of pacemaker controls symptoms driving may restart after 1 month. 1/2/3 year licence with medical review on renewal.	Recommended permanent refusal or revocation except in exceptional circumstances and where there is no other disqualification condition. Apply to DVLA.
IMPLANTATION OF DEFIBRILLATOR OR ANTI-TACHYCARDIA DEVICE	Recommended permanent refusal or revocation.	Recommended permanent refusal or revocation.
MALIGNANT VASOVAGAL SYNDROME AND CARDIOGENIC SYNCOPE	Cases individually considered by DVLA.	Cases individually considered by DVLA.

CARDIOVASCULAR DISEASE

CARDIOVASCULAR DISORDERS	GROUP I ENTITLEMENT	GROUP II ENTITLEMENT
ECG ABNORMALITY Pathological Q waves in 3 leads or more (i.e. a duration of 40 m/secs or more and the depth of at least 1/3 of the succeeding R wave). Left Bundle Branch Block (LBBB)	DVLA need not be notified unless disqualifying conditions in other sections. Till 70 retained.	(Re) Licensing permitted if no other disqualifying conditions are present and the exercise ECG requirements can be fulfilled.
PRE-EXCITATION	DVLA need not be notified unless disqualifying conditions in other sections. Till 70 retained.	May be ignored UNLESS associated with an arrhythmia (refer back to arrhythmia section).
VALVULAR HEART DISEASE Including Heart Valve Replacement NB: ANTICOAGULANT TREATMENT DOES NOT CONSTITUTE A BAR TO THE HOLDING OF A LICENCE	DVLA need not be notified, driving may continue unless disqualifying conditions in other sections. Till 70 retained.	Recommended refusal or revocation if in the past 5 years there is a history of: 1) cerebral ischaemia 2) embolism 3) arrhythmia (see below) 4) persisting LV or RV hypertrophy or dilation. Otherwise licensing will be permitted, subject to normal regular review. Where atrial fibrillation persists after valve replacement relicensing may occur 3 months after surgery provided (1), (2) and (4) above can be satisfied AND he/she is on ANTICOAGULANTS.

CARDIOVASCULAR DISEASE

CARDIOVASCULAR DISORDERS	GROUP I ENTITLEMENT	GROUP II ENTITLEMENT
HYPERTENSION	DVLA need not be notified, driving may continue unless the medication causes symptoms which will affect driving ability (see below under Drug Treatment).	Recommended refusal or revocation in uncontrolled hypertension if the casual BP is 200 systolic or greater or 110 diastolic or greater or where established BP exceeds 180 systolic or greater or 100 diastolic or greater, or medication causes symptoms which affect driving ability. Driving may restart when hypertension is controlled satisfactorily (see below under Drug Treatment), provided there are no other disqualifying conditions.
SIMPLE SYNCOPAL ATTACK(S) – PHYSIOLOGICALLY PROVOKED AND POSTURAL HYPOTENSION	Need not be notified and driving need not cease if not associated with heart disease.	As for Group I.
CARDIOMYOPATHIES (e.g. dilated hypertrophic or restrictive) HEART OR HEART LUNG TRANSPLANT	DVLA need not be notified. Driving may continue unless disqualifying conditions in other sections. Till 70 retained.	Recommended permanent refusal or revocation.

CARDIOVASCULAR DISORDERS	GROUP I ENTITLEMENT	GROUP II ENTITLEMENT
	DVLA need not be notified. Driving may continue unless disqualifying conditions in other sections. Till 70 retained.	CONGENITAL HEART DISEASE e.g. mild pulmonary stenosis, atrial septal defect, small ventricular septal defect, bicuspid aortic valve and mild aortic stenosis, patent ductus arterious, coarctation of the aorta with mild gradient and no systemic hypertension. Partial anomalous pulmonary venous drainage. Complex disorders e.g. Fallots etc. are likely to disqualify but each case is considered individually by DVLA.
MARFAN'S SYNDROME AND ALLIED DISORDERS	As above	Marfan's syndrome and allied disorders with aortic root dilatation normally will disqualify.
DRUG TREATMENT – side effects from medication likely to impair driving performance.	If causes symptoms which will affect driving ability or sudden and disabling vertigo or syncope driving must cease until satisfactory control of symptoms is achieved.	Applicants or licence holders suffering symptoms causing or likely to cause sudden impaired consciousness or significant constitutional symptoms should be regarded temporarily unfit until the symptoms have completely resolved. If symptoms are likely to be recurrent or permanent recommended refusal or revocation.

CARDIOVASCULAR DISEASE

GROUP II ENTITLEMENT ONLY

EXERCISE TESTING: STANDARD BRUCE PROTOCOL OR EQUIVALENT
(Re)licensing normally will be permitted 3 or more months after successful
rehabilitation following an event if there are no other disqualifying
*conditions, provided the applicant or driver can complete **SAFELY** at least*
the first 3 stages of the standard Bruce treadmill protocol or equivalent,
off cardio-active treatment for 24 hours and during the test remains free
of symptoms and signs of cardiac dysfunction. The licence normally will
*be **refused** if he/she develops pathological ST segment shift during or*
after the test, fails to achieve or maintain a rise in systolic blood pressure,
develops sustained ventricular tachycardia or other malignant arrhythmia
or develops symptoms attributable to peripheral vascular disease which
limits the investigation. If the identity of the chest pain is in doubt an
exercise test should be carried out as above. Those with a locomotor disorder
who cannot comply should notify DVLA.

NB: CORONARY ANGIOGRAPHY IS NOT REQUIRED.
If it has been undertaken the Licensing Authority will be recommended
to refuse or revoke the licence if it demonstrates:

   i)   *IMPAIRED LEFT VENTRICULAR FUNCTION, i.e. AN EJECTION*
       FRACTION < 40% OR,

   ii) *SIGNIFICANT (i.e. > OR = 30% REDUCTION IN INTRALUMINAL*
       DIAMETER) OCCLUSIVE DISEASE IN THE LEFT MAIN CORONARY
       ARTERY, OR SIGNIFICANT (i.e. > OR = 50% REDUCTION IN
       INTRALUMINAL DIAMETER) OCCLUSIVE DISEASE IN THE
       PROXIMAL PART OF THE LEFT ANTERIOR DESCENDING
       ARTERY ie PROXIMAL TO THE ORIGIN OF THE FIRST SEPTAL
       AND DIAGONAL BRANCHES, OR IN TWO OR MORE MAJOR
       CORONARY ARTERIES.

LICENCE DURATION – GROUP II ONLY

An applicant or driver who has, after cardiac assessment, been permitted to hold either LGV or PCV licence will be issued with a short term licence renewable on receipt of satisfactory medical reports.

5

DIABETES MELLITUS

Principal Author: Harry Keen MD FRCP*

Driver Licensing Provisions

The Road Traffic Acts require people diagnosed as having diabetes
mellitus (treated other than by diet alone) to report their condition
to the Licensing Centre. Ordinary licence holders and applicants
(Group I) *treated with **insulin*** injections must demonstrate satisfactory
control, recognise warning signs of hypoglycaemia and also not suffer
from a relevant disability. They are sent a detailed letter explaining
their requirement to report any change or deterioration which may
significantly affect safe driving to the Licensing Centre and are granted
a one, two or three year licence. On renewal they are required to make
a self declaration, which may lead to further medical enquiries.

Those managed by **diet and tablets or diet alone** are permitted to
hold or retain a till 70 driving licence, subject to not suffering from any
relevant disabilities and the need to report significant deterioration or
subsequent insulin treatment.

Group II vehicle drivers on insulin licensed before the 1 April 1991
are dealt with individually and licensing is subject to satisfactory
annual consultant medical certification, and to the proviso that they
are not suffering from any other relevant disabilities.

Since 1 April 1991 diabetic patients on insulin are barred by
law from first applying for an LGV/PCV driving licence and from
renewing thereafter.

*   *Professor of Human Metabolism, UMDS – Guy's Hospital.*

Group II drivers on diet alone or diet and tablet treatment are permitted a Group II licence, providing they do not suffer from a relevant disability or develop a need for insulin treatment.

Insulin-dependent Diabetes Mellitus (IDDM)

The classical form of diabetes, usually presenting with prominent symptoms of thirst, polyuria, weight loss and weakness, or if diagnosed late, with disturbance of consciousness, is an absolute indication for treatment with insulin by injection, hence its descriptive name. It is sometimes known as Type I diabetes and was formerly termed "juvenile onset type" diabetes. Though clinical onset is usually in youth, it may emerge at any age, even in old people. There may be a remission early in the clinical course when, temporarily, the diabetes may be controllable by tablets or even by diet alone. This "honeymoon remission" inevitably ends with an obligatory return to daily injection therapy.

The fullest possible involvement of the patient, adequately supported by educational input from the diabetes team, is necessary to obtain good blood glucose control. Modern technology enables patients to measure their own blood glucose with great simplicity and to adjust insulin dose and timing to optimise control and so minimise the risk of developing diabetic complications.

Non Insulin-dependent Diabetes Mellitus (NIDDM)

The great majority of the million or so people with diabetes in the UK are of the non insulin-dependent variety (sometimes known as Type II and formerly as "maturity-onset type" diabetes). This form of diabetes is usually diagnosed in later life and is often associated with obesity. Although non insulin-dependent in the sense that there is no absolute requirement for injected insulin to prevent severe ketoacidosis or to preserve life, a proportion of such patients come to be prescribed insulin injection treatment to obtain adequate control of their blood glucose levels. The rest are treated with dietary modification alone or with the addition of oral anti-diabetic preparations (sulphonylureas, biguanides or acarbose). Modern management requires regular systematic reviews of visual and renal function and particular attention to the prevention of tissue damage to foot and leg as well as the correction of risk factors for cardiovascular disease.

Other Forms of Diabetes

In a small number of patients, the diabetic state can be explained by accompanying disease of endocrine glands or pancreas (e.g. acromegaly, Cushing's syndrome, pancreatitis, haemochromatosis, etc.). Some of these "secondary" diabetic patients may need to be treated with insulin injections and others not; their suitability for holding a driving licence will depend upon this and upon the other effects (if any) of the underlying primary disorders. Gestational diabetes which is first diagnosed in pregnancy usually disappears after delivery and is only exceptionally insulin treated in Britain, though when this is the case, declaration to the DVLA is needed even though insulin treatment is usually temporary.

"Complications" of Diabetes

These may usefully be separated into the relatively acute metabolic complications of the disease and the longer term, delayed structural changes which develop in the eyes, kidneys, nerves and arteries.

Hypoglycaemia

Of the acute metabolic problems, hypoglycaemia is the most dramatic, significant and relevant to driving performance. There is some endocrine response when blood glucose falls below 4 mmol per litre and effect on brain function at 3.3 mmol per litre and below. It can impair co-ordination of thought and action and, if uncorrected, potentially culminate in stupor and sometimes convulsions. Clinically significant hypoglycaemia is virtually restricted to the insulin-injected diabetic. In such patients it is almost always due to a mismatch between the peaks of action of the injected insulin and the glycaemic profile of carbohydrate absorption, either in timing or in quantity. Thus, an erroneously high insulin dose with correct diet can result in hypoglycaemia as can correct dosage with inadequate, late or missed food intake. Vigorous physical exertion, especially if performed during the peak period of insulin activity, may provoke biochemical or symptomatic hypoglycaemia at the time or soon after. Liability to hypoglycaemia can be reduced by several strategies, including care with dose measurement and timing, by injecting the insulin into an area of the body unlikely to be involved in anticipated exercise (e.g. anterior abdominal wall), by care in relating the type and timing of the meal to the insulin type and dose and by altering dose levels appropriately to changing circumstances. For instance, the insulin dose may need to be increased during infective stress which evokes temporary insulin resistance. It is important to reduce the dose as the resistance declines.

Occasional slight or trivial hypoglycaemia is an expected and acceptable accompaniment of effective modern treatment, aiming as it does at the achievement of near normoglycaemia to reduce the risk of long-term diabetic complications. The educational curriculum must include patient recognition of hypoglycaemia and knowledge of prompt and appropriate correction as a priority item. The first indicators of hypoglycaemia are usually the results of activation of the sympathetic nervous system and the release of adrenalin into the circulation to counteract the falling blood glucose resulting in pallor, sweating, forceful heart beat, tremulousness and apprehensiveness in varying degree and sequence. If the low blood glucose is not raised promptly, glucose deprivation of the central nervous system (neuroglycopenia) will ensue, causing cerebral symptoms which may include double vision, confusion of thought, inappropriate behaviour and errors of judgement. If sufficiently protracted and severe loss of consciousness follows. The great majority of insulin treated people can readily recognise the first indications of hypoglycaemia and take preventive action. Self measurement of blood glucose at times of hypoglycaemic risk (e.g. late morning or afternoon and just before retiring) can help avoid hypoglycaemic episodes.

Recognition of the early signs of hypoglycaemia and a clear understanding of what to do about them is essential knowledge for the person with insulin-treated diabetes and it should be systematically and repeatedly taught. Ordinarily, getting promptly to the next meal or taking emergency sugar by mouth will meet the situation, but for vehicle drivers and others in critical situations, rigorous preventive strategies and special action are essential and effective (see below). Repeated hypoglycaemic episodes, unusual in timing, severity or manifestation are clearly serious for the patient and, if resistant to correction, require professional advice. For nocturnal hypoglycaemia, a household companion should be supplied with a glucagon injection kit and taught how and when to use it. *Patients should be reminded that insulin is a drug within the meaning of the Road Traffic Act 1988, and that a driver with symptoms of hypoglycaemia runs the risk of being charged with driving under the influence of drugs.* Some diabetic patients may become unaware of hypoglycaemic symptoms or lose "sympathetic activation" warning symptoms and develop unheralded cerebral symptoms. This loss of warning may result from a number of causes, some of them identifiable and reversible, and should be reported to the specialist responsible for the care of the diabetes. Loss of hypoglycaemic warning symptoms represents an added risk to patients themselves and, under appropriate circumstances, to others.

Rapid and delayed acting insulin preparations are available and are now widely used, often mixed together in suitable proportions in two, sometimes three or more injections per day, in many cases conveniently administered from a portable pen-type injector which can be adjusted to deliver the required dose. Day to day treatment decisions must be made by the patient if good control is to be maintained and hypoglycaemic risk minimised. Education and motivation of the patient for the acquisition and effective implementation of diabetic knowledge therefore ranks as a prime requirement of diabetes management.

Ketoacidosis

Diabetic ketoacidosis is highly unlikely to develop so fast as to constitute a threat while driving. It is not until decompensation is far advanced, usually taking many hours, that judgement might be disturbed or consciousness impaired.

Longer-term Complications

The long-term complications of diabetes require assessment on a case-by-case basis. They may progress with time. Visual problems are those most relevant to driving and result from diabetic retinopathy or cataract, rarely, from ocular or optic nerve lesions. Visual standards relating to driving safety are those applied generally. Significant deterioration in vision due to progressive retinopathy should be reported to the Licensing Authority. Widespread ablative retinal photocoagulation, used in the treatment of retinopathy, may of itself reduce peripheral vision to a significant extent and to lead to unfitness to drive (Hubert et al 1992).[1] Diabetic neuropathy may cause dense sensory deficits and uncommonly motor loss in legs and feet. Neurological and vascular deficit may result in tissue damage to feet and legs leading to chronic ulceration and amputation. When severe, these may hinder or preclude driving. Arterial disease susceptibility makes the diabetic patient a target for coronary, cerebrovascular and peripheral arterial disease and this should be assessed along the same lines as for the non-diabetic.

Car Driving and Diabetes

There are several published reports which compare the driving performance and record of people with diabetes with non-diabetics. Although some of these fail to distinguish between diabetes treated with and without insulin and some are subject to ascertainment and other biases they indicate little if any increased accident risk in diabetic drivers.

Waller (1965)[2] reported that Californian drivers with diabetes averaged twice as many accidents per million miles of driving as drivers in an age-adjusted comparison group.

Davis *et al* (1973)[3] reported a slightly higher accident rate for diabetic men than for all male drivers but found that the rate for diabetic men aged seventeen to twenty-one years was lower than for their non-diabetic counterparts.

Ysander (1970)[4] showed a reduction in the frequency of road accidents and road accidents and/or traffic offences after the onset of diabetes compared with a control series, but a high proportion of the investigated drivers (21%) especially at ages above 50 years stated that they had ceased to drive on account of the disease or its complications.

De Klerk and Armstrong (1983)[5] compared hospital admission rates for road trauma for patients with diabetes with those for the whole population. There was no overall difference but there was a significant excess in diabetic men aged under 55 arising from those in control of a vehicle and involvement of pedestrians.

Taylor (1983)[6] found that insulin treated diabetes was responsible for 17% of 1,605 police reported accidents in which the driver survived and was minimally injured to the point that he could resume driving subsequently. This was the second largest group who collapsed at the wheel. In reviewing 100 of these cases, 35% suffered from altered consciousness and 62% from complete loss of consciousness.

In the UK Clarke *et al* (1980)[7] questioned 157 insulin-treated diabetic car drivers, selected at random from two Midland diabetic clinics. Almost one-half of the men and one in five of the women admitted to hypoglycaemia (or premonitory symptoms) while driving. Only one driver in two kept rapidly available carbohydrate permanently in the car.

In the Edinburgh region (Frier *et al* 1980)[8] reported that about one-third of 250 insulin-treated patients holding driver licences had experienced significant hypoglycaemia at some time in the preceding six months. Thirteen of them (5.2%) stated that hypoglycaemia had contributed to accidents. About 43% had failed to disclose their diabetes when applying for a licence or to inform the licensing authority after developing the condition. Many of them claimed that the need to declare their diabetes was not made clear. One-third had not reported their diabetes to their motor insurers. An 8 year follow up of 232 of these patients suggested (Eadington & Frier 1989) that their accident rates (per million miles driven) were rather lower than those for the general Scottish driver population estimated from Department of Transport and motor insurance claims statistics. A substantial proportion of them had still not declared their diabetes.

Diabetes Mellitus

A leading article (Frier 1992)[9] reviews driving and diabetes in relation to a report from general practice (Saunders 1992)[10] reflecting the increase in concern with diabetes at primary health care level.

A further study of 120 unselected, fully licensed non insulin-dependent diabetic drivers from Edinburgh (Steel *et al* 1981)[11] documented the rarity of driving problems arising from this form of diabetes. Of the 65 treated with sulphonylureas, none admitted to experiencing hypoglycaemia while driving; only five had ever noted even mild hypoglycaemic symptoms. Diabetes had been declared by only 18% in their licence application. There was no excess of patients with visual disability or other diabetes-related disorder likely to impair driving skills but there was the expected excess of ischaemic heart and cerebrovascular disease. The Edinburgh group recommended that diabetic patients not treated with insulin should inform the licensing authority (a) if they started treatment with insulin injections, (b) if they developed significant complications or cardiovascular disease, (c) if they experienced hypoglycaemia on oral anti-diabetic agents, (d) if they wished to obtain vocational licences. Nevertheless, diabetes may be either "relevant" or a "prospective" disability under the Road Traffic Acts. The law requires *all* people with diabetes treated with oral agents or insulin to inform the Licensing Authority when applying for driver's licence, or later if the condition is diagnosed while a licence is held. The doctor should bring this to the attention of the newly diagnosed patient.

The driving experiences of 354 insulin-requiring diabetic in the patients in the Belfast area compared with 302 similar non-diabetic hospital control drivers was reported by Stevens *et al* (1989).[12] The proportions of the two groups admitting to one or more driving-related accidents over the preceding 5 years were very similar (23.2% diabetic drivers versus 24.8% non-diabetic drivers), rates very comparable to those reported by

Eadington and Frier (1989).[13] Of the 354 diabetic drivers, 122 had failed to declare their diabetes to the licensing centre, many mistakenly thinking that declaration was not obligatory, and approximately the same number had failed to inform their insurance companies. Of those who had stopped driving because of diabetic disabilities, the great majority had done so voluntarily rather than because of revocation of licence.

Overall, therefore, recent evidence is not suggestive of any significantly increased risk of road traffic accidents amongst diabetic drivers as a group.

Suggestions for Advice to Patients

People with diabetes starting or changing to treatment with tablets or insulin should be informed of the legal requirement to report their condition when making initial or renewal application for driver's licence. Those holding a "till 70" licence should write to the licensing authority if they develop the condition or if they have developed the condition and have not already notified it. There is evidence that many fail to do so and they risk trouble with the law and potential difficulties with insurance companies to whom diabetes must also be declared. It should be made clear that motor insurance companies may reclaim liability costs from the insured if the driver has failed to declare diabetes with major personal financial consequences particularly in the case of serious injury.

Diabetes treated with diet alone, or with diet plus metformin and/or acarbose, carries no hypoglycaemia risk, and therefore no significant driving risk (assuming of course there are no significant relevant diabetic complications). Treatment with sulphonylurea drugs however (e.g. glibenclamide, gliclazide, glipizide, etc.) can be associated with hypoglycaemia, though less commonly than with insulin, and similar (though perhaps less stringent) driving precautions should be advised.

Those diabetic patients who inject insulin (whatever the "type" of diabetes), and who are not disqualified on account of other problems, can reasonably expect support in applying for ordinary private driver's licence, provided that their diabetic condition is under reasonable control, that their understanding of diabetes and its treatment is adequate, and that they are not subject to frequent, unpredictable or sudden (without warning) attacks of hypoglycaemia. The World Health Organisation and the British Diabetic Association recommend that private car licences should be issued only when diabetic control and the level of understanding of diabetes management by the patient are adequate.

Insulin-taking diabetic car drivers must be clearly instructed to avoid hypoglycaemia at all costs while at the wheel. Driving should be avoided at times when the likelihood of hypoglycaemia is increased (e.g. just before meals or after heavy physical exertion) or additional and sufficient carbohydrate food should be eaten to remove the risk. Such diabetic drivers must at all times carry within easy reach an adequate supply of rapidly absorbed carbohydrate-rich food such as glucose tablets (Dextrosol, Boots), sugar lumps or sweets. They should also carry a card saying they are receiving insulin to facilitate resuscitation in the event of accident involvement. Drivers should always stop, by the clock, for meals and should eat additional carbohydrate *before symptoms*, if delayed by unforeseen circumstances. Drivers can and should make liberal use of the currently available simple methods for measuring their own blood glucose. If the driver experiences any of the early warning symptoms of hypoglycaemia, the vehicle must be stopped, the ignition key removed, the driving seat vacated, and adequate carbohydrate promptly consumed. Diabetic drivers should know that if they have an accident attributable to hypoglycaemia they render themselves liable to the charge of driving under the influence of drugs. Doctors should ensure that this information is known, understood and applied by their diabetic patient and should refer to it repeatedly. The British Diabetic Association's leaflet "Driving and Diabetes" contains authoritative information and advice and can be obtained together with much other material, from the **Diabetes Care Department, British Diabetic Association, 10 Queen Anne Street, London W1M 0BD**.

Vocational Drivers

Occupations not requiring special driving licences: Those who do a lot of driving in connection with their jobs, or carry special responsibility as drivers of minibuses or ambulances, but do not need supplementary licences, must not conceal their diabetes from the employer or the insurance company. In the event of an accident, failure to report it may have serious legal or financial consequences (Lister, 1983).[14]

Taxi drivers: Local authorities and metropolitan police each have their own licensing requirements, but some apply the Group II medical standards.

Group II Drivers: There is much variation in legal status and requirement for insulin taking drivers of large commercial vehicles (DiaMond Study 1993)[15] and some disputation on the additional risks involved (Songer et al 1993);[16] however in the United Kingdom the situation is clear. New applicants on insulin or existing drivers becoming insulin treated, have been barred in law from driving these groups since the 1 April 1991. However, if a person held an HGV/PSV licence on the 1 April 1991 and had previously informed the Traffic Commissioner who granted the licence, that he or she was diabetic and on insulin, then a licence may be granted subject to annual consultant certification and providing the driver does not suffer from any other relevant disability.'

DIABETES MELLITUS

REFERENCES

1. Hubert M F et al Passing the DVLC field regulations following bilateral pan-retinal photocoagulation in diabetes Eye 1992;6;456–60.

2. Waller J A (1965) Chronic medical conditions and traffic safety, N. Engl. J Med. 273 1413–1420.

3. Davis T G Wehling E H Carpenter R E (1973) Oklahoma's Medically restricted drivers – a study of selected medical conditions. Oklahoma State Medical Association Journal 66, 322–327.

4. Ysander L (1970) Diabetic motor-vehicle drivers without driving licence restrictions. Acta Chir. Scand. Supp. 409, 45–53.

5. De Klerk N H Armstrong B K (1983) Admission to hospital for road trauma in patients with diabetes mellitus. J Epidermiol. Community Health, 37, 232–237.

6. Taylor J F (1983) Epilepsy and other causes of collapse at the wheel. In driving and Epilepsy – and other causes of impaired consciousness edited by R B Godwin-Austen and M L E Espir. Royal Society of Medicine, International Congress and Symposium Series No.60 London: Academic Press Inc., and the Royal Society of Medicine. Pp 5–7.

7. Clarke B Ward J D Enoch B A (1980) Hypoglycaemia in insulin-dependent drivers Br. Med. J., 386.

8. Frier B M Steel J M Matthews D M and Duncan L J P (1980) Driving and insulin-dependent diabetes. Lancet, 1, 1232–1234.

9. Frier B. Driving and Diabetes, B M J 1992; 305 1238–9.

10. Saunders C J P. Driving & Diabetes, B M J 1992; 305: 1265.

11. Steel J M Young R J Frier B M Duncan L J P (1981(Driving and insulin-independent diabetics. Lancet 2,354–356.

12. Stevens AB, Roberts M, McKane R, Atkinson AB, Bell PM, Hayes JR. Motor vehicle driving among diabetics taking insulin and non-diabetics. Br Med J 1989; 299; 591–5.

13. Eadington D W, Frier B M Type 1 diabetes and driving experience; an eight-year cohort study. Diabetic Medicine 1989; 6: 137–141.

14. Lister J (1983) The employment of diabetics. Br. Med. J., 287, 1087–1088.

15. DiaMond Project Group Global regulations on diabetics treated with insulin and their operation of commercial motor vehicles. Br Med J 1993; 307: 250–3.

Enquiries in 24 of the countries co-operating in the WHO-sponsored DiaMond study showed great variation in national practice with regard to the licensing of people with insulin-requiring diabetes to drive heavy commercial vehicles. Eight countries (including Japan and Finland) permit licensing without restriction; 10 (including several European countries) do not permit licensing at all; 6 issue driving licences but with substantial restrictions.

16. Songer T J Lave L B LaPorte R E The risks of licensing persons with diabetes to drive trucks. Risk Anal 1993; 13: 319–26.

DIABETES MELLITUS

DIABETES MELLITUS	GROUP I ENTITLEMENT	GROUP II ENTITLEMENT
INSULIN TREATED Diabetic drivers are sent a detailed letter of explanation about their licence and their medical condition by DVLA.	Must demonstrate satisfactory control, recognise warning symptoms of hypoglycaemia and meet required visual standards. 1/2/3 year licence. Confirmation on renewal of satisfactory health.	New applicants on insulin or existing drivers becoming Insulin treated are barred in law from 1/4/91. Drivers licensed before 1/4/91 on Insulin are dealt with individually and licensing is subject to satisfactory annual Consultant certification.
MANAGED BY DIET AND TABLETS Diabetic drivers are sent a detailed letter of explanation about their licence and their medical condition by DVLA.	Subject to satisfactory medical enquiries will be able to retain Till 70 licence unless develop relevant disabilities e.g. diabetic eye problems affecting visual acuity or visual field or insulin required.	Review of medical condition. Drivers will be licensed unless they develop relevant disabilities e.g. diabetic eye problem affecting visual acuity or visual fields, in which case either recommended refusal or revocation or short period licence. If becomes insulin treated recommended refusal or revocation.
MANAGED BY DIET ALONE Diabetic drivers are sent a detailed letter of explanation about their licence and their medical condition by DVLA.	Need not notify DVLA unless develop relevant disabilities e.g. diabetic eye problems affecting visual acuity or visual field or insulin required.	Drivers will be licensed unless they develop relevant disabilities e.g. diabetic eye problem affecting visual acuity or visual fields, in which case either recommended refusal or revocation or short period licence.

DIABETES MELLITUS

DIABETIC COMPLICATIONS	GROUP I ENTITLEMENT	GROUP II ENTITLEMENT
Loss of awareness of Hypoglycaemia	If confirmed driving must stop. Driving may resume provided reports show awareness of hypoglycaemia has been regained, confirmed by Specialist report.	See above for insulin treated. Recommended permanent refusal or revocation.
Frequent hypoglycaemia episodes or poor diabetic control	Cease driving until satisfactorily control re-established, with Specialist report.	See above for insulin treated. Recommended permanent refusal or revocation.
Eyesight complications (affecting visual acuity or fields)	See Section: VISUAL DISORDERS	See above for insulin treated and Section: VISUAL DISORDERS.
Renal Disorders	See Section: RENAL DISORDERS	See Section: RENAL DISORDERS.
Limb Disability	See Section: PHYSICAL DISABILITY	As Group I.
Gestational Diabetes	NOTIFY DVLA if Insulin treatment instituted. MUST meet requirement above and inform DVLA if Insulin treatment continuing after delivery.	NOTIFY DVLA. Legal bar to holding a licence while insulin treated. Re-apply following delivery provided not on insulin.

6

EPILEPSY

Principal Author: Professor David Chadwick DM MA FRCP*

Background

Epilepsy is the commonest neurological disorder. It has a prevalence of between 0.5 and 1% of the population and on average an incidence of 50 per 100,000 of the population throughout life (Hauser & Hesdorfer, 1990). Peak incidence is in childhood and adolescence and in later life when cerebrovascular disease becomes an important cause of epilepsy. Surveys of general practice populations of patients with epilepsy in the United Kingdom indicate that approximately 1% of a general practice population has a history of seizures in the last two years or is currently taking anti-epileptic drugs and has a previous history of seizures. Of these at least 50% have been seizure free for periods of time in excess of 1 or 2 years but are continuing to take anti-epileptic drugs (Goodridge and Shorvon, 1983, Jacoby et al, 1993). Very often the decision to continue taking anti-epileptic drugs after significant periods of remission of seizures is motivated by the fear of further seizures affecting the ability to drive (MRC Study of Anti-epileptic Drug Withdrawal, 1991). Until recently British driving licence authorities (DVLA Swansea) required the majority of people declaring epilepsy who could meet the regulations to have a driving licence restricted to three years duration. However, the work by Chadwick (see later) has recently resulted in a new policy to grant till age 70 licences to those drivers with epilepsy who have been free from seizures for 6 years and have no risk of progressive epilepsy.

*   *Department of Neurological Science, The Walton Centre for Neurology and Neurosurgery, Rice Lane, Liverpool L9 1AE.*

EPILEPSY

People with a history of seizures and epilepsy have their driving restricted because it is generally believed that such drivers would be at increased risk of having accidents. Such a risk would be expected to increase due to a susceptibility to sudden episodes of loss of consciousness whilst driving or due to the consumption of anti-epileptic drugs which are known to have some effects on cognitive function including concentration and motor reaction times. Few studies have addressed accident rates in drivers with a history of epilepsy in a scientifically acceptable way (Naughton and Waller, 1980, Waller, 1965, Crancer and McMurray, 1968, Hansotia and Broste, 1991). None has given satisfactory information about clinical aspects of the epilepsy in the drivers studied, in particular how remote was the last seizure from the time of the survey. The highest relative risk identified was 1.95 (Waller, 1965). A more recent study suggested a relative risk of 1.33 in a population of 434 patients (Hansotia & Broste, 1991). It is striking that these relative risks of accidents do not differ from risks for other less strictly regulated chronic medical conditions such as diabetes (Waller, 1965) and that variables such as age and sex may have a much greater influence on accident risks in non-epileptic populations (Maycock et al, 1991). The contribution of epilepsy related accidents to the overall incidence of accidents is difficult to ascertain. A study from the Netherlands found that 1 accident in 10,000 and 1 fatality in 10,000 traffic deaths was attributed to seizures whilst driving (van der Lugt, 1975). On the other hand of 2000 police reported accidents due to drivers collapsing at the wheel but surviving, Taylor, (1989) found that the largest number were due to epileptic seizures. Excluding first seizures, 71% of the people collapsing at the wheel due to epilepsy had failed to declare their condition in relation to their driving licence. 11% of accidents were due to a first seizure and might therefore be regarded as unpreventable.

EPILEPSY

Shortly to be published work by Chadwick and Taylor (1995) reviews the accident rate by questionnaire of 17,000 British drivers declaring epilepsy to the Licensing Authority (DVLA) and comparing it to that of 8,000 randomly selected drivers. Drivers with epilepsy have about the same overall road traffic accident involvement as controls but with more casualties requiring hospital admission beyond 24 hours. Drivers with epilepsy also have greater involvement in fatal road traffic accidents.

The Current Regulations

In successive Road Traffic Act Regulations since 1960, epilepsy is specified as one of the "prescribed disabilities" which means that anyone suffering from epilepsy is barred from holding a driving licence. However in regulations regarding the granting of driving licences to people with epilepsy the bar has been lifted, first in 1969 and most recently in 1994. Currently epilepsy remains a prescribed disability under Section 92(3)b, but if it is controlled, then a licence may be granted for 1, 2 or 3 years provided that the person satisfies the following conditions:

a) he shall have been free from any epileptic attack during the period of one year immediately preceding the date when the licence is to have effect; OR

b) he shall have had an epileptic attack whilst asleep more than 3 years before the date when the licence is granted and shall have had attacks only whilst asleep between the date of that attack and the date when the licence is granted; and

c) the driving of a vehicle by him in pursuance of the licence is not likely to be a source of danger to the public.

The broad intention is to grant ordinary driving licences to people with epilepsy who have been free from any attacks for one year, with or without treatment, or who have a history of at least three years of attacks only during sleep. In addition to the above, licence holders are required by law to inform the Driver and Vehicle Licensing Centre (DVLC) Swansea at once "if you have any disability (which includes any physical or mental condition) that is or may become likely to affect your fitness as a driver, unless you do not expect it to last for more than three months".

Medical Advice

The regulations do not differentiate in any way between tonic clonic seizures on the one hand and less severe seizures on the other (e.g. the aura of epileptic seizure which is in fact a simple partial seizure; a brief absence or myoclonic jerks). Thus the persistence of even minor symptoms relating to epileptic seizures can continue to prevent an individual with a history of epilepsy obtaining a driver's licence.

Because of these complexities it is of the utmost importance that drivers with a history of epilepsy or being diagnosed as having epilepsy for the first time should, as part of the counselling process, not only be given a full and complete account of the relationship of their epilepsy to the symptoms that they have suffered, but also be counselled carefully about the driving regulations. A licence holder or potential applicant who develops epilepsy, should be told by his doctor quite clearly that he has epilepsy and that the law will prohibit him from driving. It must be emphasised to him that he is required by law to inform the DVLA as soon as possible. It is important that drivers understand that continued driving under these circumstances will be illegal and may invalidate any comprehensive motor insurance cover that the individual might have or result in an insurer reclaiming third party costs from the driver. The driver should also, however, understand that their doctor has no legal responsibility to inform the DVLA and that responsibility lies solely with the patient. Doctors counselling patients would be well advised to keep a written record of the fact that the counselling has taken place. It is important that patients understand that the DVLA is the body with statutory authority to withdraw a licence and that the doctor's only responsibility to his patient under these circumstances is to make sure that the patient is satisfactorily informed. Concealment of epilepsy and symptoms of epilepsy is common and it is important for the best medical care of patients that they are not in any way confused by the fact that their doctor's main concern in the future will be control of seizures and that a full and frank disclosure by the patient to the doctor represents the best form of ongoing care.

It is of great importance that all doctors responsible for diagnosing epilepsy are fully aware of the driving regulations with respect to the condition. It is clear that in the past considerable confusion has existed (Harvey and Hopkins, 1983). Certainly the current UK regulations can be criticised on the grounds that relying on patient notification often results in poor compliance. In a recent study only 27% of 661 patients counselled by neurologists in the UK complied with the regulations to disclose information about first seizures, epilepsy and other unexplained loss of consciousness to the DVLA (Taylor et al, 1994). However, systems of regulation that demand the doctor notify driving agencies, as exist in some US States, creates considerable problems for the doctor patient relationship and the ability to manage optimally a person's epilepsy.

With regard to confidentiality, doctors should observe the code of professional conduct; but – if judged to be in the best interests of the patient or the public, and if every effort to obtain the patient's compliance or consent has failed –

the doctor should disclose confidential information (SEE CHAPTER 2, PART 2).

The assessment of whether driving by someone who has had epileptic attacks is "likely to be a source of danger to the public", i.e. condition (c) in the current regulations, is often a very subjective matter, but the application of this condition may be relevant in those who have had epileptic attacks and who also have low intelligence, have psychological disturbances or other evidence of a persistent cerebral disorder. In such cases, even though freedom from fits may exceed one year, it may be judged that condition (c) cannot be fulfilled and that driving should be barred.

It is important that drivers understand that the periods of remission that lead to a licence being granted are not specifically related to whether or not anti-epileptic drugs are being taken, as patients who continue to take anti-epileptic drugs can continue to drive once they have achieved one year seizure free. However a more difficult position arises in drivers who have achieved a remission and have continued drugs but then decide that they would wish to withdraw them. The withdrawal of anti-epileptic drugs in such circumstances carries with it on average a 40 to 50% risk of seizure recurrence in the succeeding 2 years, but most of this risk occurs during the period of dosage reduction and during the withdrawal and within 6 months of stopping anti-epileptic drug therapy (MRC Anti-epileptic Drug Withdrawal Study, 1991). Under these circumstances most patients with a driving licence should be advised not to drive for 6 months after discontinuing therapy. They should be aware that the recurrence of seizures on withdrawal of therapy will result in a further revocation of their licence until they again achieve a seizure free period of 1 year.

EPILEPSY

An Isolated Seizure

It is not uncommon that doctors see patients who give a history of a single seizure or a single seizure episode in which 2 or more seizures occur during a 24 hour period. Most authorities would agree that such people cannot be said to be "suffering from epilepsy" but they clearly are at higher risk of seizures in the future than are a normal population of people. The risk for seizure recurrence after single seizures varies widely across a number of different studies (Chadwick, 1991). US studies provide low estimates of the risk of seizure recurrence (30% by 2 years) whereas most new case studies indicate considerably higher risks of up to 80%. These differences probably reflect different policies of treating single seizures with anti-epileptic drugs on the two sides of the Atlantic. Certainly the institution of anti-epileptic drug treatment after a single seizure approximately halves the risk of seizure recurrence (FIRST Group, 1993). When an isolated seizure is diagnosed it is again essential that drivers are informed of their legal responsibilities to inform the DVLA. Usually a licence will be revoked until a seizure free period of 12 months has been attained.

In some circumstances seizures may clearly be provoked (acute symptomatic seizures). Where the provocation is unlikely to recur patients may be allowed back to driving at an earlier date but should still inform the DVLA. Where acute symptomatic seizures occur because of abuse of alcohol or other drugs, such abuse will be the most important factor determining if and when a licence will be reissued.

There are rare circumstances in which the occurrence of a single seizure may lead to the full epilepsy regulation being applied. One of these is the finding in an EEG of generalised 3 Hz spike wave activity. Childhood absence epilepsy is unique in that there is a correlation between the presence of an EEG abnormality and the occurrence of seizures, and every burst of such abnormal activity in the EEG must be viewed as a seizure. In these terms patients with such 3 Hz spike wave activity can no longer be regarded as only having suffered a single seizure. It should be emphasised that childhood absence commonly remits by early adult life and that faster spike wave seen in juvenile absence and juvenile myoclonic epilepsy would not result in the application of the full epilepsy regulations. For this reason abnormalities in the EEG are exceptionally unusual reasons for the full epilepsy regulations to be applied following a single clinical seizure.

The other situation where a clinical seizure may lead to the application of the full epilepsy regulations is where investigation of such a seizure reveals the presence of a clear structural cause (e.g. cerebral tumour, previous cerebral infarction or cerebral abscess).

There are some situations in which the prospective risk for the development of epilepsy following severe head injury or craniotomy are such that driving is prohibited for a period of time. These conditions are dealt with elsewhere (see Chapter 7).

Seizures Starting Only During Sleep

The current regulations allow a small number of people with epilepsy who continue to have epileptic seizures to drive if the seizures are restricted to sleep. It is well recognised that seizures with localised onset in the brain (partial seizures) have a predisposition to occur during sleep and any epileptic seizure occurring during sleep must be regarded as having a localised onset (Janz, 1961). Whilst there is always some risk that seizures during wakefulness will also occur this risk probably diminishes the longer fits remain restricted to sleep (Gibberd and Bateson, 1974). However it is of great importance when explaining these regulations to patients to ensure that a full history is taken to exclude the possibility that epileptic auras (simple partial seizures) or relatively mild complex partial seizures are occurring during the day. Those whose epilepsy presents with seizures whilst asleep must stop driving until either they have been free of all attacks for 1 year or the attacks have occurred only whilst asleep over a period of 3 years immediately preceding the date on which the licence is to be granted. It needs to be emphasised that the regulations apply to seizures occurring during sleep and not to "nocturnal epilepsy". Not all nocturnal attacks occur during sleep and attacks whilst asleep can occur during the daytime. Any person who holds a licence on the basis of this regulation must be advised to stop driving if any seizure occurs whilst awake.

Unexplained Episodes of Loss of Consciousness

The diagnosis of an epileptic seizure or seizures can only be made on the basis of a clear history from the patient and an eyewitness. Inevitably one or more events may occur that lead unequivocally to altered awareness or loss of consciousness but for which there is inadequate clinical information on which to base a definite diagnosis. Such episodes nevertheless have clear implications for continued driving irrespective of whether or not they have occurred at the wheel of a car. It is important that patients with such undiagnosed episodes are counselled about informing the DVLA. The usual advice in such circumstances will be the withdrawal of licence until 12 months have elapsed since the last such episode.

Sudden Attacks of Disabling Giddiness or Fainting

Fainting is a common cause of loss of consciousness. Where a diagnosis of reflex vasovagal syncope can be made this should not be any impediment to driving, as it is exceptionally unusual for such syncope to occur whilst seated. However, other causes of syncope (cardiological cause including arrhythmias and valvular heart disease) can result in sudden attacks of disabling giddiness or fainting which are a prescribed disability leading to a bar to driving and which must be disclosed to a licence holder. Severe episodes of vertigo with sudden onset would similarly be covered by the regulations.

Epilepsy and Group II Entitlement

Stricter regulations apply to vocational licence holders. The regulations with respect to these licences was changed with effect from the 1st January, 1993. Previously any epileptic attack after the age of 5 would prohibit such licences being held. This has been amended so that such licences can be granted once there is no continued "liability to epileptic seizures". Such liability has been defined by the Secretary of State's Honorary Medical Advisory Panel on driving and disorders of the nervous system as having been free of all:

a) epileptic attacks for at least the last 10 years; AND

b) having not taken anti-epileptic medication during this 10 year period; AND

c) do not have a continuing liability to epileptic seizures. The last requirement would exclude any persons who have structural intracranial lesion that has previously caused seizures.

It is particularly important that holders of such group 2 licences understand the regulations clearly. Compared to car drivers vocational drivers have about 12 times the risk of accidents because of the large number of miles they drive and the possibility of serious consequences of accidents are greater (Taylor, 1983). It is particularly for this group of drivers that doctors may have to consider breaching the usual rules of confidentiality and informing the licencing authorities if one of their

EPILEPSY

patients, having been counselled, continues to drive on such a licence. Disclosure to the licencing authorities should only occur however after the doctor is certain in his own mind that there is a significant risk to the patient and public in their continued driving and after the doctor has sought advice from a medical defence society or other professional association (see Chapter 2, Part 2).

REFERENCES

Chadwick D. (1991). Why are so few patients with epilepsy treated surgically? A UK perspective. Acta Neurochirurgica Suppl. 50:117–118.

Crancer A. and McMurray L. (1968). Accident and violation rates of Washington's medically restricted drivers. JAMA, 205:74–79.

First Seizure Trial Group (FIRST.) (1993). Randomised clinical trial on the efficacy of anti-epileptic drugs in reducing the risk of relapse after a first unprovoked tonic-clonic seizure. Neurology 43:478–483.

Gibberd F. B., and Bateson M. C. (1974). Sleep epilepsy: its pattern and prognosis. Brit. Med. J. 2, 403–405.

Goodridge D. M. G. and Shorvon S. D. (1983). Epileptic seizures in a population of 6,000. Brit. Med. J., 287, 641–647.

Hansotia P. and Broste S. K. (1991). The effect of epilepsy or diabetes mellitus on the risk of automobile accidents. N. Engl J Med. 324:22–26.

Harvey P. and Hopkins A. (1983). Views of British Neurologists on epilepsy, driving and the law. Lancet 1:401–404.

Hauser W. A. and Hesdorffer D. C. (1990). Epilepsy: frequency, causes and consequences. Demos Publications, New York.

Jacoby A., Baker G., Chadwick D. and Johnson A. (1993). The impact of counselling with a practical statistical model on patients' decision-making about treatment for epilepsy: findings from a pilot study. Epilepsy Research, 16:207–214.

Janz D. (1961). Conditions and causes of status epilepticus. Epilepsia 2:170–175.

Maycock G., Lockwood C. R. and Lester J. F. (1991). The Accident Liability of Car Drivers. Department of Transport TRRL Report RR315. Transport and Road Research Laboratory, Crowthorne.

Medical Research Council Anti-epileptic Drug Withdrawal Study Group (1991). Randomised study of anti-epileptic drug withdrawal in patients in remission. Lancet 337:1175–80.

Naughton T. J. and Waller J. (1980). Feasibility of developing a medical condition collection system for driver licensing. Washington, DC: National Highway Safety Administration. US Dept. of Transportation publication, DOT HS 805–595.

Taylor J., Chadwick D. W. and Johnson A. (1994). Notification rates, driving and accident experience in people with recent seizures, epilepsy or undiagnosed episodes of loss of consciousness.

Taylor J.F. (1989) Driving & Epilepsy in Fourth International Symposium on Sod. Valproate & Epilepsy Ed. By David Chadwick Royal Society of Medicine, International Congress of Symposium Series No. 152 Royal Society of Medicine London & New York. Pages 270–273.

van der Lugt P. J. M. (1975). Traffic accidents caused by epilepsy. Epilepsia 167:747–751.

Waller J.A. (1965). Chronic medical conditions and traffic safety. N Engl J Med. 273:1413–1420.

EPILEPSY

EPILEPSY	GROUP I ENTITLEMENT	GROUP II ENTITLEMENT
EPILEPSY: *Diagnosed/confirmed* Whatsoever the clinical seizure type. Epileptic attacks occurring at the wheel are currently the most frequent and important preventable medical cause of road traffic accidents. NB: If within a 24 hour period, more than one epileptic attack occurs, they are treated as a "single event", for the purpose of applying the epilepsy regulations.	THE EPILEPSY REGULATIONS APPLY. Provided a licence holder/applicant is able to satisfy the regulations normally a 3 year licence will be issued. Till 70 restored if 6 years seizure free and there is no progressive risk of fits. *See overleaf for full regulations.*	THE EPILEPSY REGULATIONS APPLY. On 1.1.93 the previous regulation was amended to 'A liability to epileptic seizures'. If this is demonstrated the licence must be refused or revoked. *See overleaf for full regulations.*
FIRST EPILEPTIC SEIZURE/SOLITARY FIT ALSO SEE UNDER 1. fits associated with misuse of alcohol or misuse of drugs whether prescribed or illicit 2. neurosurgical conditions.	ONE YEAR OFF DRIVING WITH MEDICAL REVIEW BEFORE RESTARTING DRIVING. Review licence for 1/2/3 years. Till 70 restored after 6 years provided no further attack. (Special consideration may be given when the epileptic attack is associated with certain clearly identified non-recurring provoking cause).	See the section above dealing with Epilepsy.
WITHDRAWAL OF ANTI-EPILEPTIC MEDICATION AND DRIVING	See * overleaf for guidance.	See * overleaf for guidance.

EPILEPSY

EPILEPSY	GROUP I ENTITLEMENT	GROUP II ENTITLEMENT
PROVOKED SEIZURES (apart from alcohol or illicit drug misuse).	See ** overleaf for guidance.	See ** overleaf for guidance.
LOSS(ES) OF CONSCIOUSNESS, IN WHICH INVESTIGATIONS HAVE NOT REVEALED A CAUSE i.e. there is an open ended liability for recurrence, and the cause is unexplained.	With a single episode at least one year off driving with freedom from such attacks during this period. Review licence for 1/2/3 years. Till 70 after 4 years (i.e. treated as for solitary fit).	Recommended refusal or revocation. After 5 years, freedom from such episodes, specialist assessment may be undertaken to decide when driving may restart.

The Current Epilepsy Regulations for Group I and Group II Entitlement

GROUP I

The Motor Vehicles (Driving Licences) Regulations 1987, as amended by SI 1994 No. 1862, prescribes epilepsy as a relevant disability for the purposes of Section 92(2) of the Road Traffic Act 1988. This means that:

a) A person who has suffered an epileptic attack whilst **awake** must refrain from driving for **one** year from the date of the attack before a driving licence may be issued; and

b) A person who has suffered an attack whilst **asleep** must also refrain from driving for **one** year from the date of the attack, unless they have had an attack whilst asleep more than three years ago and have not had any awake attacks since that asleep attack.

c) In any event, the driving of a vehicle by such a person should not be likely to cause danger to the public.

(The amending Regulations as regards to epilepsy came into effect from 5 August 1994).

NB: If Epilepsy or a first fit has been diagnosed, and 3 per second spike and wave activity subsequently remains present on EEG the person will be regarded as continuing to suffer from epilepsy, and the epilepsy regulations will apply.

GROUP II

The amending Regulations for Group II entitlement came into effect from 1 January 1993; 'an epileptic attack since attaining the age of five years' amended to:

"A liability to epileptic seizures" which is prescribed as a relevant disability for the purpose of the Road Traffic Act in relation to Group II (LGV/PCV) licences. Thus the prerequisite is that such a liability has been, or can be demonstrated prospectively.

The Secretary of State's Honorary Medical Advisory Panel on Driving and Disorders of the Nervous System recommend that this liability – be assessed – in persons with a history of epileptic attacks or seizure by the ability to meet all of the following criteria:

have been free of epileptic attack for at least the last ten years

have not taken anti epileptic medication during this ten year period

do not have a continuing liability to epileptic seizure

The last requirement would exclude persons who have some structural intracranial lesion thus increasing the risk of seizure.

EPILEPSY

DVLA Guidance Letter Sent to Practitioners Advising a Driver to Withdraw Anti-epileptic Medication on Specific Medical Advice

We understand from driving licence medical enquiries that your patient is to discontinue or has discontinued treatment for epilepsy within the previous 6 months. From a medico-legal point of view, may we draw your attention to the potential risk of further epileptic seizures which may occur during this therapeutic procedure. If an epileptic seizure does occur, the Law will not permit your patient to continue to hold a licence until the driver or applicant is able to satisfy the Regulations in regard to Epilepsy and Driving. These currently require a period of 1 year free of any manifestation of epileptic seizure or attacks occurring whilst awake, but special consideration is given where sleep only attacks have occurred.

It is clearly recognised that withdrawal of anti-epileptic medication is associated with a risk of seizure recurrence. A number of studies have shown this, including the randomised study of anti-epileptic drug withdrawal in patients in remission, conducted by the Medical Research Council Anti-epileptic Drug Withdrawal Study Group. This study shows 40% increased associated risk of seizure in the first year of withdrawal of medication compared with those who continued on treatment.

The Secretary of State's Honorary Medical Advisory Panel on Driving and Disorders of the Nervous System has recommended that patients should be warned of the risk they run, both of losing their driving licence and also of having a seizure which could result in a road traffic accident. The Panel recommend that patients should be advised not to drive from commencement of the period of withdrawal and thereafter for a period of 6 months after cessation of treatment. The Panel consider that a person remains as much at risk of seizure associated with drug withdrawal during the period of withdrawal as in the 6 months after withdrawal. It is up to the patient to comply with such advice. Clearly for DVLA to revoke the licence during the period of withdrawal would be both restrictive and unnecessarily bureaucratic.

As your patient may wish to discuss this matter with you, a letter is being sent to your patient with a copy of this letter.

It is important to remember that if medication is withdrawn, e.g. on admission to hospital for non epileptic conditions, and epileptic seizures occur, that the person will be required to meet the epilepsy regulations.

**Provoked Seizures

For Group I and possibly Group II drivers or applicants, provoked or symptomatic seizures, apart from those caused or precipitated by alcohol or illicit drug misuse, will be dealt with on an individual basis by DVLA. For provoked seizure(s) with alcohol or illicit drugs please see relevant section in the booklet. Doctors may wish to advise patients that the period of time likely to be recommended off driving will be influenced inter alia, by:

a) Whether a "liability to epileptic seizures" has been demonstrated, or precipitated specifically as a result of the provoked episode and,

b) Whether the provoking or precipitating factor(s) has been successfully or appropriately treated or removed.

Such cases might include reflex anoxic seizures, seizures with medication e.g. tricyclics et alia, immediate seizure at time of acute head injury or neurosurgical operation, at onset of acute stroke or TIA or during acute exacerbation of neurological disorders e.g. with MS.

7

EPILEPSY AND NEUROSURGICAL DISORDERS

Principal Author: Professor Bryan Jennett CBE MD FRCS*

Current regulations for driving when there is a risk of epilepsy concentrate on the likelihood of further seizures once the diagnosis of epilepsy has been made – because one or more seizures have already occurred. When these have happened in association with provocation such as recent cerebral trauma (accidental or surgical) there is often hesitation to make the diagnosis of epilepsy, although there is a substantial risk of recurrence. On the other hand some patients recovering from recent brain damage can be identified as at high risk of developing epilepsy, even though no seizure has yet occurred; they have a "relevant disability".

About 5% of patients admitted to hospital after recent head injury have a seizure in the first week (early epilepsy), and about 5% have epilepsy later, with some patients having both (Jennett 1975). Seizures in the first week are often limited to focal twitching and less than a third of affected patients go on to have late fits, whilst most patients who have a late seizure continue to be liable to seizures. The risk of late epilepsy varies greatly according to the type of injury and early complications. Factors predisposing to late traumatic epilepsy are an intracranial haematoma that is surgically removed within 2 weeks of injury (35% risk) and a depressed fracture of the skull vault (15% risk). When an intracerebral haematoma is seen on CT scanning but surgical evacuation is not required the risk of epilepsy is only about 20%. The epilepsy risk after chronic subdural haematoma evacuated through burr holes is low. After compound depressed fracture of the skull vault the risk of epilepsy varies from 1–60% according to various combinations of risk factors

*   *Emerit. Prof of Neurosurgery, University of Glasgow.*

(see figure 1) whether the dura is torn, there is more than 24 hours PTA, there are focal neurological signs of cortical damage or there has been early epilepsy. In patients who have neither a depressed fracture nor an intracranial haematoma the risk of late epilepsy is only about 1%, even if there is prolonged PTA, unless there has been an early seizure. When there has been a seizure in the first week after injury in such cases the risk of later epilepsy is about 25%.

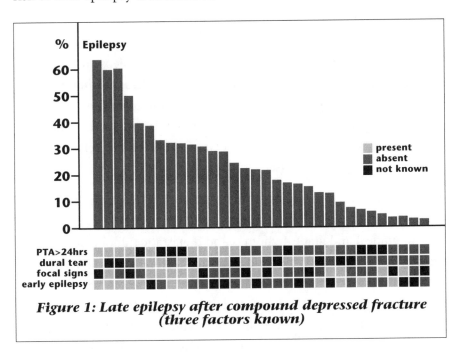

Figure 1: Late epilepsy after compound depressed fracture (three factors known)

Data about the frequency of epilepsy after craniotomy for non-traumatic conditions is now available from several authors (Foy et al 1981 a, b; Gautier Smith 1970; Jennett 1987). In patients with no previous seizures craniotomy has about a 20% risk of late post-operative epilepsy, whether the lesion is benign or malignant tumour or intracerebral haemorrhage. With previous seizures the risk is double this. Cerebral abscess carries a very high risk of epilepsy.

EPILEPSY AND NEUROSURGICAL DISORDERS

After craniotomy for ruptured aneurysm the epilepsy risk is about 20% if there is any post-operative neurological deficit but about 10% for middle cerebral aneurysms without deficit, and quite low for other sites without deficit (Jennett 1994). Prophylactic anti-convulsants in patients at risk of post-traumatic or post-operative epilepsy appear to confer little benefit according to several well conducted trials (North et al 1983, Temkin et al 1990, Foy et al 1992).

Suggested Advice

After head injury associated with early epilepsy, the epilepsy regulations should apply (one year off driving etc. Group I), unless the only seizure occurred immediately at the time of injury. After injuries associated with a high risk of epilepsy, but no seizures so far, no driving is recommended until the risk has fallen below 20% for Group I drivers and below 2% in the case of Group II drivers (see table opposite).

After craniotomy for benign supratentorial intracranial tumours, a year off driving is advised, whilst for grade I and grade II gliomas two years and for grade 3 and grade 4 gliomas and metastatic tumours four years. After craniotomy for anterior and posterior cerebral artery aneurysms with neurological deficit, six months off driving is recommended but driving may be resumed on clinical recovery where there is no deficit. In the case of aneurysms of the middle cerebral artery with a neurological deficit, 12 months off driving is recommended and 6 months without deficit.

Epilepsy other than an immediate attack at the time of the bleed requires application of the epilepsy regulations. Group II drivers are regarded unfit unless specialist assessment has determined that the epilepsy risk is no more than 2%.

Patients at risk from epilepsy due to brain damage associated with injury or surgery frequently have other mental or physical disabilities that affect their competence to drive. These include abnormalities of behaviour that can influence decision-making and judgement, particularly under conditions of stress; physical disabilities of vision, hearing and motor performance are also important. For some conditions such as subarachnoid haemorrhage or malignant intracranial tumour there is also the risk of recurrence of the primary pathological condition. One or more of these factors may render a driver unfit even though the risk of epilepsy is acceptably low.

Initial % Risk of Epilespsy	1	2	3	4	5	6	7	8	9	10	Years after injury
6%	3	2	1.5	1							
10%	5	3	2.5	2	1.5	1					
15%	7	5	4	3	2.5	2	1				
20	10	7	5	4.5	3.5	3	2	1.5	1		
25	13	9	7	6	5	4	2.5	2	1.5	1	
30	16	12	9	7.5	6	5	3	3	2	1	
35	19	14	11	9	7.5	6	4	3.5	2.5	1.5	
40	23	17	13	11	9	7	5	4.5	3	2	
45	27	20	16	14	11	9	6	5	4	2	
50	31	24	19	16	13	11	7	6.5	5	3	
55	35	28	22	19	16	13	9	8	6	3.5	
60	40	32	26	22	18	15	11	10	7	4	

Residual % risk of epilepsy occurring after years of fit-free interval after different initial risk levels for craniotomy head injury patients (Jennett 1988).

Group I driving is NOT recommended until the risk of fits is below 20% and Group II driving until the current risk of fits is below 2%

For example a head injury victim with an initial risk of epilepsy of 35% would not be able to drive group II until 10 years after injury.

REFERENCES

Foy PM, Copeland GP and Shaw MDM. (1981). The incidence of post-operative seizures. Acta Neuro Chir 55: 253–64.

Foy PM, Copeland GP and Shaw MDM. (1981). The natural history of post-operative seizures. Acta Neuro Chir 57: 15–22.

Foy PM, Chadwick DW and Rajgopalan N et al. (1992). Do prophylactic anti-convulsant drugs alter the pattern of seizures after craniotomy? J Neurol Neurosurg Psychiat 55: 753–57.

Gautier Smith PC. (1970). Parasagittal and falx meningiomas. London: Butterworth.

Jennett B. (1975). Epilepsy after non-missile head injuries. 2nd ed. London: Heinmann.

Jennett B. (1987). In Epilepsy: Hopkins A, Ed. London: Chapman and Hall.

Jennett B. (1994). In Epilepsy: Hopkins A, Ed. 2nd ed. London: Chapman and Hall.

North JB, Penhall RK, Hamieh A et al. (1983). Phenytoin and post-operative epilepsy: a double blind study. J Neurosurg 58: 672–77.

Temkin NR, Dikmen SS, Wilensky AJ et al. (1990). A randomised double blind study of phenytoin for the prevention of post-traumatic seizures. New Engl J of Med 323: 497–502.

EPILEPSY AND NEUROSURGICAL DISORDERS

NEUROSURGICAL DISORDERS	GROUP I ENTITLEMENT	GROUP II ENTITLEMENT
EPILEPSY/EPILEPTIC SEIZURES General guidance for ALL neurosurgical conditions if associated with epilepsy or epileptic seizures	In all cases where epilepsy has been diagnosed the epilepsy regulations must apply. These cases will include all cases of single seizure where a primary cerebral cause is present and the liability to recurrence cannot be excluded. An exception may be made when seizures occur at the time of an acute head injury or intracranial surgery.(see pages 2/3)	In all cases where a "liability to epileptic seizures" either primary or secondary has been diagnosed the specific epilepsy regulation for this group must apply. The only exception is a seizure occurring immediately at the time of the acute head injury or intracranial surgery, and not thereafter and/or where no liability to seizure has been demonstrated. (see pages 2/3)
BENIGN SUPRATENTORIAL TUMOUR e.g. meningioma, intracranial cyst et al SURGICAL TREATMENT BY CRANIOTOMY	One year off driving, then 3 year licence. Till 70 restored after 4 years if no recurrence.	Recommended refusal or revocation. New application may be considered, provided at least 10 years since surgery, with evidence of complete removal or cure. Specialist assessment may be required.
BENIGN INFRATENTORIAL TUMOUR (POSTERIOR FOSSA) e.g. acoustic neuroma, meningioma (et al) SURGICAL TREATMENT EXCEPT BY CRANIOTOMY	Resume driving following recovery and retain Till 70 licence.	As for Group I provided no residual disabling symptoms.

EPILEPSY AND
NEUROSURGICAL DISORDERS

NEUROSURGICAL DISORDERS	GROUP I ENTITLEMENT	GROUP II ENTITLEMENT
PITUITARY TUMOUR	PROVIDED NO VISUAL FIELD DEFECT (IF VISUAL FIELD LOSS SEE VISION SECTION).	PROVIDED NO VISUAL FIELD DEFECT (IF VISUAL FIELD LOSS SEE VISION SECTION).
SURGICAL TREATMENT CRANIOTOMY	Resume driving when clinically recovered, Till 70 restored after 4 years.	6/12 months off driving.
TRANSPHENOIDAL SURGERY	Drive following recovery. Retain Till 70.	As for Group I.
OTHER TREATMENT (e.g. Radiotherapy) or untreated.	Drive following recovery. Retain Till 70.	As for Group I.
MALIGNANT INTRACRANIAL TUMOURS		
Grade 1	1 year off driving.	Recommended permanent refusal or revocation.
Grade 2 and 3	At least 2 years off driving, restoration of the licence will depend on no evidence of new activity.	Recommended permanent refusal or revocation.
Grade 4 or cerebral secondary deposits.	Normally 4 years off driving – some individuals in very exceptional cases may be invited to reapply for assessment after 2 years.	Recommended permanent refusal or revocation.
MALIGNANT INTRACRANIAL TUMOURS IN CHILDREN WHO SURVIVE TO ADULT LIFE WITHOUT RECURRENCE	Normally Till 70 licence.	Individual assessment: see above as for 'benign intracranial tumour'.

EPILEPSY AND NEUROSURGICAL DISORDERS

NEUROSURGICAL DISORDERS	GROUP I ENTITLEMENT	GROUP II ENTITLEMENT
SERIOUS HEAD INJURY operated acute intracerebral haematoma or compound depressed fracture with dural tear or with more than 24 hours post traumatic amnesia. ALSO SEE UNDER: 1. Intracranial haematoma 2. Personality disorders 3. Burr hole surgery 4. Driving assessment for disabled drivers	Six months off driving. But 1 year if craniotomy. Where consciousness was lost but with none of the complications specified in the first column and clinical recovery is full and complete, driving may resume without notifying DVLA.	Recommended refusal or revocation. Specialist assessment to determine if and when driving may restart, depending on significant reduction of prospective epilepsy risk, and to ensure driving performance not likely to be impaired.
INTRACRANIAL HAEMATOMA Extradural – requiring craniotomy but NO cerebral damage	6/12 months off driving.	1 year off driving.
Extradural – requiring craniotomy and with cerebral damage	1 year off driving.	Recommended refusal or revocation. Return to driving will depend on Specialist assessment (when epilepsy risk is approx. 2%).
Acute Subdural – burr holes – Craniotomy	6 months off driving. 1 year off driving.	Recommended refusal or revocation. Return to driving will depend on Specialist assessment (when epilepsy risk is approx. 2%)
Chronic Subdural	Resume driving on recovery.	6 months – 1 year off depending on features.

EPILEPSY AND NEUROSURGICAL DISORDERS

NEUROSURGICAL DISORDERS	GROUP I ENTITLEMENT	GROUP II ENTITLEMENT
INTRACRANIAL HAEMATOMA (continued) Acute Intracerebral		
– burr holes	Six months off driving.	Recommended refusal or revocation. Return to driving will depend on Specialist assessment (when epilepsy risk is approx. 2%).
– Craniotomy	1 year off driving.	
SUBARACHNOID HAEMORRHAGE (see also intracranial haematoma) 1. DUE TO INTRACEREBRAL ANEURYSM a) SURGERY CRANIOTOMY Anterior or posterior cerebral aneurysm		
With NO deficit	Driving permitted when clinically recovered from craniotomy.	Recommended refusal or revocation. Specialist assessment to determine when driving may start – when epilepsy risk is no more than 2%.
With deficit	6/12 months off driving. Till 70 restored after 4 years if no complications.	
Middle Cerebral Aneurysm		
With NO deficit	Driving permitted 6/12 months after craniotomy.	
With deficit	1 year off driving.	

NEUROSURGICAL DISORDERS	GROUP I ENTITLEMENT	GROUP II ENTITLEMENT
SUBARACHNOID HAEMORRHAGE (continued)		
b) OTHER TREATMENT e.g. Embolisation and all other non-craniotomy procedures	Cease driving until full clinical recovery. 1/2/3 year licence with regular medical review. Till 70 restored after 4 years if no complications.	Recommended refusal or revocation. Must demonstrate lesion completely ablated with no residual abnormal vessels. Specialist assessment (including comprehensive normal angiography) to determine if and when driving may restart.
c) NO TREATMENT i.e. Aneurysm present but no intervention	6/12 months off driving then Till 70 if no complications.	Recommended permanent refusal or revocation.
d) INCIDENTAL FINDINGS OF INTRACRANIAL ANEURYSM (no history of subarachnoid haemorrhage)		
NO TREATMENT	Retain Till 70 licence. Resume driving on recovery. Till 70 restored after 4 years.	Recommended refusal or revocation because or risk of haemorrhage. Specialist assessment if driving wished to be resumed, to assess risk of haemorrhage.
SURGERY CRANIOTOMY		Recommended 1 year off driving.

EPILEPSY AND
NEUROSURGICAL DISORDERS

NEUROSURGICAL DISORDERS	GROUP I ENTITLEMENT	GROUP II ENTITLEMENT
2. DUE TO INTRACRANIAL ARTERIOVENOUS MALFORMATION (Angioma/AVM which have bled)		
a) SURGERY CRANIOTOMY	1 year off driving. Review licence with Till 70 restored after 4 years.	Recommended refusal or revocation. If completely removed or ablated, Specialist assessment to determine if and when driving may restart.
b) OTHER TREATMENT (Embolisation or stereotactic radiotherapy)	Cease driving until satisfactory recovery. 1/2/3 year licence with regular medical review. Till 70 restored if completely ablated.	Recommended refusal or revocation. Must demonstrate lesion completely ablated with no residual abnormal vessels. Specialist assessment to determine if and when driving may restart.
c) NO TREATMENT i.e. Angioma present but no intervention	Cease driving until full clinical recovery. 1/2/3 year licence issued initially.	Recommended permanent refusal or revocation.
d) INCIDENTAL FINDING OF INTRACRANIAL AVM/ANGIOMA (no history of subarachnoid haemorrhage)		
NO TREATMENT	1/2 or 3 year licence issued initially.	Recommended refusal or revocation because of risk of bleed and epilepsy with Specialist assessment as to if/when might ever resume driving.
SURGICAL/OTHER TREATMENT	Period off driving depending on type of treatment (if any) – see section 2 a, b above.	Recommendation depending on type of management – see 2 a, b above.

EPILEPSY AND NEUROSURGICAL DISORDERS

NEUROSURGICAL DISORDERS	GROUP I ENTITLEMENT	GROUP II ENTITLEMENT
3. NO CAUSE FOUND	Provided comprehensive cerebral angiography normal – resume driving following recovery. Till 70 licence.	Recommended 6/12 off driving. Provided comprehensive cerebral angiography normal: 6/12 off driving and may regain licence if symptom free.
CEREBRAL ABSCESS	Two years off driving as high risk of developing epilepsy. Then 1/2/3 year licence with medical review. Till 70 after 5 years if no epileptic attack.	Recommended refusal or revocation. Very high prospective risk of epilepsy. May consider if 10 years from treatment and no seizure.
HYDROCEPHALUS	If uncomplicated, Till 70 licence.	Can be issued with a licence if uncomplicated and no associated neurological problems.
INTRAVENTRICULAR SHUNT Insertion of or revision of upper end of V.P. shunt

INTRACRANIAL PRESSURE MONITORING DEVICE Inserted by Burr hole surgery.(The prospective risk from the underlying condition must be considered also. | Recommended 6/12 off driving after shunt insertion, then 1/2/3 year licence. If symptom free 5 years, Till 70 restored. | Assessment required, cases considered individually. |

8

EXCESSIVE SLEEPINESS

Principal Author: Professor J D Parkes MD, FRCP*

Introduction

Excessive wake-time sleepiness is common. Population studies in the USA, Finland and Israel suggest a prevalence between 3.7% and 4.2%.[1,2,3] Several recent surveys highlight the problem of falling asleep at the wheel, as a factor in road traffic accidents and emphasise that excessive sleepiness is a major health problem.[4,5,6] Leger estimates that sleepiness and sleep disorders have been underestimated as a cause of road accidents in comparison with alcohol and drug abuse. However, these latter may also be associated with sleepiness.[7,8] Sleepy drivers may not be aware that they have a problem and several studies show that train drivers can operate a train for several minutes after falling asleep.[9]

Causes of Excessive Sleepiness

Excessive sleepiness is most commonly **secondary** to *fatigue, persistent insomnia, shiftwork,*[10] *burning the candle both ends, drugs and alcohol.* Even a short sleep loss for one hour each night for a prolonged period has a cumulative effect on wake time performance.[8]

Primary causes are Symptomatic sleep apnoea – has a prevalence in middle age men of about 1% with 0.3% requiring treatment; the *narcoleptic syndrome* is a lifetime illness with prevalence of 5 per 10,000; *the upper airways resistance syndrome* has an uncertain prevalence but may at least be as common as the narcoleptic syndrome; *head injury* is an important cause of excessive sleepiness, the incidence of common

*   *Professor of Clinical Neurology, University Dept of Neurology, Institute of Psychiatry and Kings College, London.*

causes of excessive sleepiness such as persistent insomnia and sleep apnoea increase with age.

Circadian Rhythm of Vigilance and Sleep

During the daytime, there is a period of low vigilance and sleep tendency from 1400–1700 hours. In subjects who remain awake at night there is a period of sleep tendency from around 0200 to 0700 hours. These normal vigilance changes are exaggerated in persons with excessive sleepiness and Mitler et al (1988).[11,12] has shown that they may have major public health consequences in major industrial accidents such as the Chenobyl and Three Mile Island nuclear power disasters and the Challenger Space Shuttle catastrophe.

Motor Accidents and Sleep

The United States National Highway Transportation Safety Administration's road traffic accidents statistics for 1990 indicate that daytime sleepiness was a major factor responsible for 1% of the total of 57,000 crash reports.[13] 96% of these accidents involved a passenger vehicle, 4% truck drivers. 77% were male and the peak time of crash was between midnight and dawn, most involved a single vehicle only.

Surveys of people with sleep disorders who drive indicate that between 30% and 90% had fallen asleep whilst driving, the exact frequency depending on the pathology. Patients with sleep apnoea have a seven fold increase in risk of car accidents.[14] Between 40% to 48% narcoleptic drivers reported falling asleep whilst driving, whilst 25% of these had accidents related to sleepiness.[15]

Figures from the USA may not be directly comparable with those in the UK. Horne reported a survey by Leicestershire police on a British motorway suggesting that sleepiness may have been responsible for 20% of accidents.[16]

Diagnosis of Excessive Sleepiness

An accurate clinical history is the most important diagnostic pointer. Important clinical criteria are:

1 obstructive sleep apnoea

- excessive daytime sleepiness

- loud snoring, honking, respiratory obstructive noises during sleep usually most severe in prone posture

- observed prolonged breath holding periods during sleep (over 10 sec but often 30–60 sec)

- severe motor restlessness during sleep (common but not invariable)

- obesity (only 60% of subjects)

2 narcoleptic syndrome

- cataplexy: anticipation of laughter causes paralysis and loss of muscle tone with "jelly" attacks accompanied by flickering of face muscles. The presence of unequivocal cataplexy is essential for diagnosis.

- persistent excessive daytime sleepiness (essential for diagnosis)

- insomnia (present in 80% of subjects)

- short sleep latency at night (bedtime-sleep onset 1–2 minutes) (present in 80% of subjects)

- reported dreams at sleep onset (present in 60% of subjects)

3 "idiopathic" hypersomnolence

- persistent excessive daytime sleepiness

- prolonged (over 8h) night sleep without arousals

- difficulty in morning arousal

- no cataplexy

4 upper airways resistance syndrome

- excessive daytime sleepiness

- continuous snoring

- diagnosis made by finding of multiple brief arousals accompanying snoring on sleep laboratory studies without apnoea and without oxygen desaturation.

Measurement of Daytime Sleepiness

Measurement of excessive sleepiness depends on subjective and objective tests. These include simple self rating scales such as the Epworth Sleepiness Scale,[17] which can be used in the clinical as well laboratory-based measurement of different aspects of performance (e.g. driving skills).

Sleep laboratories do a number of physiological tests designed to measure sleepiness. These include the multiple sleep latency test (MSLT) which measures the time taken to fall asleep under standard conditions on five occasions at 2h intervals throughout the day[18] the maintenance of wakefulness test (MWT[19]) and recently, EEG alpha power spectral analysis over a fixed time period.

The results of the MSLT and MWTV tests depend on the set, setting and the nature of the attempted task. The results of the different tests do not always correlate well with actual driving performance but give a useful measure of the propensity to, or the severity of, excessive sleepiness.

Suggestions for Advice to Patients

- Anyone subject to wake-time sleepiness shouldn't drive.

- Alcohol even in small doses may lead to somnolence and an accident.

- Sedative-hypnotics are best avoided by drivers.

- It is essential to early diagnose and treat sleep disorders. More often such patients may be labelled "lazy", "workshy" or "bored" when in effect they have a potentially life threatening medical disorder if they drive.

- Health screening at primary care level should combine a simple rating scale (such as the Epworth Sleepiness Scale above) with a sleep-wake log kept by the patient for 2–4 weeks. Such a procedure is also useful to monitor the result of subsequent treatment.

- Drivers with a diagnosed sleep disorder who are driving licence holders must be advised of the requirement to notify DVLA. They should be warned that failure to notify is a criminal offence and may also have serious financial motor insurance consequences. Treatment which prevents a sleep disorder from manifesting itself does not exempt the need for notification.

- Doctors should warn their patients about the possible driving consequences of a sleep disorder.

- Drivers who have successfully been treated and have advised DVLA accordingly should be warned to avoid overlong journeys, especially on motorways and, as far as possible, to avoid driving at night.

- It should be stressed that 80% of patients with sleep apnoea, the narcoleptic syndrome and upper airways resistance syndrome can be treated successfully with restoration of normal or near normal wake time alertness.

- Specialist advice from a sleep disorder centre should be sought wherever necessary.[20]

- In subjects on treatment, a period of observation to evaluate the effectiveness is often necessary before reassessing driving ability. In sleep apnoea, response to positive pressure treatment is often dramatic and rapid but in up to 50% of patients compliance may lapse.

In the narcoleptic syndrome it can take between 4–10 weeks to establish the optimum dose of central stimulants. One-third of subjects develop tolerance to the alerting effects of amphetamine over 3–12 months. If tolerance develops, central stimulant drugs rotation may be necessary.

THE PERIOD OF DRIVING RESTRICTION DEPENDS ON THE PERIOD NEEDED TO ESTABLISH NORMAL ALERTNESS, THIS VARIES FROM CASE TO CASE.

Group II Drivers

Group II driving buses or goods vehicles generally involves considerably longer time spent at the wheel and many haulage drivers spend long hours driving at night. Large Goods Vehicles have approximately three times the fatality rate per mile travelled as do cars, whilst Passenger Carrying Vehicles have approximately four times the car fatality rate. The medical referees in the Drivers Medical Unit at DVLA consider each case individually in conjunction with reports obtained from the doctors and specialists involved in the case. They have to be satisfied, on behalf of the Secretary of State, as licensing authority that any necessary treatment is effective and the patient is likely to be compliant. Where these two conditions cannot be met, Group II licensing is withheld.

REFERENCES

1. Coleman RM Diagnosis, treatment and follow-up of about 8,000 sleep-wake disorder patients In Guilleminault C Leugaresi E ed. Sleep-wake disorders natural history, epidemiology and long-term evolution.

2. Patinen M Kaprio J Koskenvuo M Langinvainio H Sleep habits, sleep quality and use of sleeping pills: a population study of 31,140 adults in Finland ibid. 29–36.

3. Lavie P Sleep apnoea in industrial workers ibid. 127–136.

4. Bixler E Kales A Soldatos C Kales K Healey S Prevalence of sleep disorders: survey of the Los Angeles Metropolitan area Am J Psychiatry 1979 136 1257–63.

5. Findley L J Fabrizio M Thommi G Surat PM Severity of sleep apnoea and automobile crashes New England Journal of Medicine 1989 320 868–896.

6. Findley L J Unverzagt ME Surat PM Automobile accidents involving patients with obstructive sleep apnoea American Reviews of Respiratory Disease 1988 138 337–340.

7. Leger D The cost of sleep-related accidents: a report for the National Commission on Sleep Disorders Research Sleep 1994 17 84–93.

8. Social Security Bulletin 1989 52 34–41 Death and Cases – State and Provincial Workers' Compensation Authorities for calendar or fiscal year costs.

9. Torsvall L Akerstedt T Sleepiness on the job: continuously measured EEG changes in train drivers. Electroencephalography and Clinical Neurophysiology 1987 66 502–511.

10. Akerstedt T Sleepiness as a consequence of shift work Sleep 1988 11 1734.

11. Mitler MM Carskadon M Czeisler CA Dement WC Dinges DF Graeber RC Catastrophes, sleep and public policy: consensus report Sleep 1988 11 100–9.

12. US Nuclear Regulatory Commission Investigations into the March 28 1979 Three Mile Island Accident by the Office of Inspection and Enforcement Investment Report No 50–320. July 1979, NTIS NUREG-0600 Washington DC: US Government Printing Office 1979 79–101.

13. Gartner NH Nelson DC Intelligent vehicles and highway systems to improve driver performance and safety In: Proceedings of the International Conference on Sleep in the Diseased Brain Jerusalem May 13–17 1994 p9.

14. George CF Nickson PQ Hanly PJ Miller TW Kryger MH Sleep apnoea patients have more automobile accidents Lancet 1987 2 447.

15. Broughton R Ghanem Q The impact of compound narcolepsy on the life of the patient In: Guilleminault C Dement WC Passouant P eds. Narcolepsy New York Spectrum Publications 1976 201–220.

16. Horne J New Scientist 4 January 1992.

17. Johns MW A new method for measuring daytime sleepiness:
The Epworth sleepiness Scale Sleep 1991 14 6 540–545.

18. Carskadon MA Guidelines for the multiple sleep latency test
(MSLT): a standard measure of sleepiness Sleep 1986 9 519–524.

19. Mitler MM Gujavarty S Bowman CP Maintenance of wakefulness
test: a polygraphic technique for evaluating treatment efficacy in
patients with excessive somnolence Electroencephalography
Clinical Neurophysiol 1982 53 658–661.

20. Sleep Apnoea and related conditions Royal College of Physicians
Working Party Report 1993 London pp 51.

9

DISORDERS OF THE
NERVOUS SYSTEM

Principal Authors: Christopher Earl MD FRCP[¥]
and Graham Wetherall MB BCh[*]

It can be in no way surprising that disturbances of functions of the brain, spinal cord or peripheral nerves may interfere with the ability to drive a motor vehicle safely. The nervous system may fail to function intermittently as in epilepsy, or there may be persistent disturbances of function, which may be fixed and unchanging, remittent or steadily progressive.

Advice of Holders of Group I Licences

CEREBRAL PALSY

In patients with cerebral palsy there is significant and unchanging loss of normal function of one or more limbs but such patients are usually able to drive safely with appropriate instruction and specially adapted vehicles. Unfortunately some patients with cerebral palsy have a liability to epilepsy which will prevent them from holding a licence unless the attacks are successfully controlled (see Chapter 6).

SPINAL CORD INJURIES

Patients with traumatic spinal cord lesions have a degree of disability which is usually static over many years and except for those where the lesion is very high in the spinal cord, can usually drive an adapted vehicle safely.

¥   *Hon. Consultant Phys. Neurology Dept, Middlesex Hospital,*
     National Hospital for Neurology and Neurosurgery & Moorfields Eye Hospital.
*   *Medical Advisor, DVLA, Swansea.*

STROKE AND TRANSIENT ISCHAEMIC ATTACKS

Strokes are a frequent cause of persistent disability. They also develop very rapidly in a way that may be a cause of danger in a patient who is driving at the moment of onset of the illness. Fortunately, accidents caused by stroke occurring while patients are actually driving are uncommon. Driving should cease for at least one month following a stroke of any sort. In the absence of epilepsy or significant impairment of mental function, Group I driving may be resumed once the physical recovery of power and sensation in the limbs is adequate to allow control of a vehicle. It is important to remember that visual field defects are often associated with strokes and may constitute a serious disability in respect of driving even when there has been satisfactory recovery of function of the limbs (see Chapter 11). Less commonly, patients may have impaired visual attention to one side (usually the left) even when the fields to ordinary testing by simple methods may show no abnormality. Where some residual disability persists in the function of the limbs, it is unlikely that minor degrees of weakness or loss of co-ordination will to cause problems with driving. Patients with more severe disturbances of limb control require practical assessment by a Mobility Centre (See Annex II). A purely expressive dysphasia would not prevent ordinary driving but difficulty in understanding oral or visual instructions could clearly cause significant risk. Personality changes may follow strokes and aggressive, impulsive or indecisive behaviour may increase the risk of accidents. The assessment of the risk in such cases is extremely difficult. Often such symptoms are brought to the attention of the doctor by the patient's family or friends who come to the doctor asking his help in preventing the patient from driving. Such observations from family or friends should be taken very seriously and they may be invited to express their concern directly to the medical adviser at DVLA. The onset of a stroke may be associated

DISORDERS OF THE NERVOUS SYSTEM

with an attack of epilepsy which may be directly due to the sudden disturbance of brain function. An attack of this sort does not necessarily imply a persistent liability to seizures. However, epileptic attacks occurring during convalescence or thereafter will make the patient subject to the ordinary rules applied to patients suffering from epilepsy (see Chapter 6).

ATTACKS OF TRANSIENT CEREBRAL ISCHAEMIA

Episodes of transient cerebral dysfunction related to ischaemia of a temporary sort may clearly cause a risk in drivers. Patients who experience such attacks should be advised not to drive until four weeks have passed after the last episode. Where there are repeated episodes, cessation may occur spontaneously or as a result of treatment. It is sometimes very difficult to distinguish between transient ischaemic episodes and attacks of focal epilepsy. This is true especially of episodes of transient ischaemia in which the only symptoms are sensory.

DEMENTIA

The assessment of drivers with dementia poses special problems, the scale of which will increase in the future as the average age of the driving population rises. A recent study of Alzheimer's disease (Drachman and Swearer 1993) showed that in the first two or three years after diagnosis, the risk of an accident was comparable with that of a driver under 25 years of age. They concluded that in general, a patient able to cope with day to day needs, retaining adequate insight and judgement, and not disorientated in time and space may be fit to drive. Where possible, friends and relatives should be asked for their opinion and if the patient is allowed to drive, a licence should be issued on a yearly basis with reassessment at each renewal. In doubtful cases,

DISORDERS OF THE NERVOUS SYSTEM

a detailed assessment by a Mobility Centre (See Annex II) will be necessary and where there is serious doubt a medical adviser at the DVLA may require a driving test to be taken.

In some cases the patient from lack of insight due to his disease may be unable or unwilling to appreciate the need to take the advice he is given. Where this is the case his medical adviser may need to take the responsibility of informing the DVLA. In doing so where the doctor believes there is a likelihood of serious danger to the patient or others his conduct would be in accordance with the guidelines on professional confidence laid down by the General Medical Council.

MULTIPLE SCLEROSIS

Weakness and lack of co-ordination of movement are the important causes of disability in multiple sclerosis. Visual symptoms (impaired visual acuity or diplopia) at some time in the course of the disease are very common but they are usually temporary. Where the doctor is uncertain about the risk involved it is appropriate that such patients should be referred for special testing and for advice about adaptations to vehicles (Annex II). The fluctuating course of multiple sclerosis may mean that frequent reassessments of the patients ability may be needed. The patient should certainly be advised not to drive during an exacerbation of the disease and may need advice when the exacerbation is over, about the time when it is safe to resume driving. Mental changes are well recognised in multiple sclerosis but are unlikely to cause problems until the later stages of the disease by which time physical disability will be the determining factor in decisions about driving. Tonic spasms are an uncommon but well recognised feature of the disease. They have been described as non-epileptic seizures. They may be very frequent (many times a day) and cause a sudden but brief stiffening and loss of use of an upper or lower limb on one side. They respond readily to treatment with carbamezapine and in any case the bouts of spasms clear spontaneously after some weeks. While occurring they certainly make driving dangerous. When they have ceased, either spontaneously or with treatment, driving may be resumed after the patient has been free of attacks for four weeks.

PARKINSON'S DISEASE

A high proportion of patients treated over many years with preparations containing levodopa will develop problems with fluctuating control of symptoms or abnormal movements. Unpredictable sudden "on-off" episodes, freezing attacks or involuntary movements may cause a driver to be considered unfit to drive, until where it is possible, control has been regained. It would be reasonable to allow a patient to drive once such disabling symptoms have been absent for three months. As Parkinson's disease progresses, some patients may develop apathy and slowness of thought which may progress to frank dementia, which may also affect the patient's ability to drive. In a doubtful case a driving assessment will be of value.

MOTOR NEURONE DISEASE

This condition affects muscular strength progressively as a result of degeneration of motor nerve cells in the brain stem and spinal cord. Generally, fitness to drive will depend on the degree and distribution of muscular weakness and the patient may be helped by the use of an appropriately adapted vehicle. The condition is a progressive one and therefore assessment may need to be repeated at intervals. The frequency of review will depend on the rate of deterioration which is very variable.

DISORDERS OF THE NERVOUS SYSTEM

POLIOMYELITIS AND MUSCLE DISEASE

The late effects of poliomyelitis and effects of primary muscle disease causing loss of muscle strength may clearly lead, in some cases to difficulties in driving. Each case will need individual assessment. In the case of muscle disease which may be progressive, repeated assessments may be necessary (See Annex II).

VERTIGO

Vertigo is a common condition and would rarely be severe enough to make driving unsafe. Whether a patient should be advised to stop driving will depend on the doctor's judgement of the severity and frequency of the attacks and it is difficult to lay down rigid criteria.

SYNCOPE

Simple syncope is not usually regarded as a reason for withdrawal of a driving licence. Sycopal attacks related to disturbances of cardiac rhythm however can cause a loss of consciousness without warning. These are dealt with in the chapter relating to heart disease. Cough syncope which is a condition which occurs in patients with obstructive airways disease in which a paroxysm of coughing will lead to loss of consciousness can clearly be dangerous, and patients who have suffered from cough syncope are unfit to drive unless the condition can be treated successfully. Micturition syncope in men occurring whilst they are standing voiding urine is no bar to driving.

VENTRICULAR SHUNTS

Drivers who have had ventricular shunts inserted for the treatment of hydrocephalus must be advised to cease driving for at least six months to ensure that the risk of suffering an epileptic seizure falls to a safe level. Where procedures are undertaken to revise the extracranial portion of a shunt, there need be no restriction on driving.

PITUITARY TUMOURS

Patients with tumours of the pituitary may present with disturbances of vision and these may make driving unsafe. Where pituitary tumours are treated surgically by the transphenoidal route, the patient may resume driving when he has recovered from the operation, provided there is no significant field loss. Drivers who have had a pituitary tumour removed at craniotomy should not drive until free from an unacceptable risk of epilepsy (See Chapter on Neurosurgery).

GROUP II LICENCES

In general, patients with progressive and disabling neurological conditions are unfit to hold a Group II licence. Thus patients with a persistent disturbance of neurological function as a result of brain injury, Parkinson's disease or multiple sclerosis should not hold a Group II licence. Those who suffer from a stroke or an episode of transient cerebral ischaemia within five years or who suffer from dementia of any degree should also be regarded as unfit. Muscular weakness of more than minor degree will prevent the holding of a licence for this group. Communication is essential in the event of an emergency and profoundly deaf people, who are unable to communicate on the telephone even with modern electronic aids if available, will not meet the medical standards required for holders of a Group II licence. Amanrosis Fugax affecting one eye before the age of 50 is no bar if cardiac and neurosurgical investigations are negative. A single episode of transient global amnesia also does not preclude Group II driving.

DISORDERS OF THE NERVOUS SYSTEM

REFERENCES

1. Driving & Alzheimer's Disease: The Risk of Crashes –
   Drachan & Swearer – 'Neurology' December 1993; 43: 2448–2456.

NEUROLOGICAL DISORDERS	GROUP I ENTITLEMENT	GROUP II ENTITLEMENT
CHRONIC NEUROLOGICAL DISORDERS e.g. Parkinson's disease, MS, muscle and movement disorders including motor neurone disease likely to affect vehicle control because of impairment of co-ordination and muscle power. See also Driving assessment for disabled drivers.	Provided medical assessment confirms that driving performance is not impaired, may retain Till 70 licence. May require licence to be restricted to "with controls to suit the disability". If condition is likely to progress rapidly or if the diagnosis is recent a short period licence of 1/2 or 3 years will be issued.	Recommended refusal or revocation if condition is progressive or disabling. If driving would not be impaired and condition stable, may be licensed subject to 1 year review.
LIABILITY TO SUDDEN ATTACKS OF DISABLING GIDDINESS AND FAINTING e.g. Meniere's disease, Labyrinthine or other brain stem disorders.	Cease driving on diagnosis. Driving will be permitted when satisfactory control of symptoms achieved. Review 1/2/3 year licence. If remains symptom free for 4 years, Till 70 restored.	Recommended refusal or revocation if condition disabling. If condition stable, must be symptom free and completely controlled for at least 1 year before re-application.

NEUROLOGICAL DISORDERS	GROUP I ENTITLEMENT	GROUP II ENTITLEMENT
CEREBROVASCULAR DISEASE: including stroke due to occlusive vascular disease, spontaneous intracerebral haemorrhage and transient cerebral ischaemia (both cerebral and ocular).	At least one month off driving after the event. When clinical recovery is fully satisfactory driving may restart. May be issued with unrestricted Till 70 licence provided there is no significant residual disability. If residual limb disability, restricted licence issued endorsed "with controls to suit the disability", and Till 70 restored (The driver receives separately an explanatory letter "Driving and Strokes" from DVLA).	Recommended refusal or revocation. Provided recovery has been full and complete and 5 years free of recurrence, specialist assessment may be undertaken to determine whether driving may restart, i.e. the driver is not considered at exceptional risk of further vascular event either cerebral or coronary, and driving performance is not likely to be impaired.
Recurrent and frequent attacks NB: Epileptic attacks occurring within the 24 hours of the acute episode are not required to meet the Epilepsy regulations. Epileptic attacks occurring outside this period will be required to meet the Epilepsy regulations. See also driving assessment for disabled drivers.	Driving should cease until the attacks have been controlled for at least 3 months.	Refusal/Revocation.
Amaurosis Fugax	As TIA.	Driving should cease. Drivers under age 50 with a single episode and investigations demonstrating NO cardiac, vascular or haematological disease may be considered for Vocational Driving. Drivers over age 50 – as TIA.

DISORDERS OF THE NERVOUS SYSTEM

NEUROLOGICAL DISORDERS	GROUP I ENTITLEMENT	GROUP II ENTITLEMENT
ACUTE ENCEPHALITIC ILLNESSES AND MENINGITIS	1) If no seizures may restart driving, when clinical recovery is complete. 2) If associated with seizures, during acute febrile illness, recommended off driving for at least 6 months from the date of seizures.3) If associated with seizures during or after convalescence will be required to meet EPILEPSY REGULATIONS See page 3.	1) As for Group I provided no residual disabling symptoms, and clinical recovery is complete. (2) and (3) Must stop driving, notify DVLA and meet current EPILEPSY REGULATIONS before driving resumes. See page 3.
TRANSIENT GLOBAL AMNESIA	Provided epilepsy, any sequelae from head injury and other causes of altered awareness have been excluded, no restriction on driving. DVLA need not be notified Till 70 retained.	A single confirmed episode is not a bar to driving, the licence may be retained. If two or more episodes occur, driving should cease and DVLA be notified. Specialist assessment required to exclude all other causes of altered awareness.

10

MENTAL DISORDERS

Principal Author: Dr Jonathan Chick MA MPhil FRCPE FRCPsych*

Psychiatric illness and driving accidents

Psychiatric illness slightly increases the risk that a driver will be involved in a road traffic accident, but this is mostly accounted for by anxiety, dementia, to a less extent depression, and of course alcoholism. Distractibility and poor concentration impede driving skills. Panic attacks have led drivers to leave the vehicle – in the case of a London bus driver this occurred on Westminster Bridge at rush hour causing considerable disruption to his passengers and the traffic.

Psychotic illness in general has not been associated with an increased accident rate, though mania has led to dramatic instances of speeding. Very occasionally suicidal intent is implicated in a crash.

Learning Disability – Mental Handicap

Stable mildly mentally handicapped people can be capable drivers. However "severe mental impairment" (in Scottish terminology "mental deficiency") of a degree which renders the person incapable of living an independent life or guarding himself against serious exploitation is an absolute bar to the holding of a licence within the European Community. (Few if any persons with this condition are capable of learning to drive.)

Personality and Behavioural Disorders

People with personality disorders are probably responsible for more accidents than those with all other mental and physical disorders

*   *Consultant Psychiatrist, Edinburgh Royal Hospital.*

combined. Aggressiveness, impulsiveness, intolerance of others and driving regardless of significant alcohol consumption are all aspects of personality disorders.

Drug treatment of mental disorders in drivers

Care needs to be taken to prescribe treatment that impairs driving as little as possible. (Among antidepressants, the newer compounds (selective serotonin reuptake inhibitors – SSRI's) cause less daytime sedation at therapeutic dosage than the traditional tricyclics.)

It is wise to advise a period of two-three weeks off driving until the effect of a new or changed psychotropic medication can be assessed. Neuroadaptation to the daytime sedative effects of psychotropic drugs commonly develops, but is not guaranteed. Carefully balanced therapy can improve rather than diminish safe driving. However patients must be warned of the somnolent effect of medications particularly on long monotonous drives, and to avoid alcohol.

Section 4 of the 1988 Road Traffic Act makes it a criminal offence for a person to drive under the influence of drugs. Drugs in this context include prescribed medicines taken in the correct dose. Falling asleep is no defence against a charge of dangerous driving.

Professional Driving

Special consideration has to be given to those who drive professionally – not only large goods vehicle and passenger carrying vehicle drivers but also taxi drivers, firemen, ambulance and police drivers. The Royal College of Psychiatrists (1993) have recently revised their recommendations for drivers of Group II vehicles, taking account of the EU directives.

"Specific psychiatric considerations for drivers of LGV's and PCV's: The Royal College of Psychiatrists recommends that:

1) An acute psychosis, whether schizophrenic, manic depressive, other depressive psychosis, or other psychosis listed in the International Classification of Diseases 10th Revision under the following categories: F20, F22, F23, F25, F28, F29, F30, F31, F32.3 and F33.3, should lead to the withdrawal of an LGV/PCV licence.

2) Dependence on alcohol or continuing chronic alcohol consumption with inability to refrain from drinking and driving, and drug abuse with dependence on psychotropic substances should lead to advice to the patient to inform the Driver Vehicle Licensing Authority (DVLA) and discontinue driving in the meantime. After a three year period of abstinence from alcohol and subject to authorised medical opinion and regular medical check-ups, the EU Directive 91/439 allows the issue or renewal of a licence for applicants or drivers who in the past have been dependent on alcohol.

3) Driving licences of any category including cars shall not be issued to or renewed for applicants who regularly use psychotropic substances, in whatever form, which hamper the ability to drive safely where such large quantities are absorbed that they are likely to have an adverse effect on driving. This shall apply to all other medicaments or combinations of medicaments which can hamper the ability to drive safely. The Royal College of Psychiatrists advises that an individual LGV or PCV licence holder or applicant should be recommended to notify DVLA about their condition and should be recommended to discontinue driving until symptom free for a period of six months.

4) Organic brain disorder leading to a psychiatric disability which might impair driving skills should be an absolute bar.

5) *Any person who has a driving licence withdrawn or withheld on medical grounds in England and Wales has a right of appeal to a Magistrates Court and in Scotland to a Sheriffs Court. An informal procedure already exists involving the Senior Medical Adviser at DVLA, with two independent psychiatrists, one nominated by the patient or the patient's general practitioner, and the other nominated by the Department of Transport.*

6) *Unless either a minimum period of three years after the cessation of treatment, or a period of three years with a stable condition whilst on medication has elapsed, an application for the reinstatement of the licence should be unlikely to receive psychiatric support. Where, following the cessation of treatment there are residual symptoms of the illness which have been stable for a minimum period of three years and do not impair driving skills, these will usually not preclude an application for the reinstatement of a licence.*

7) *Patients who have had their licence refused or revoked as a result of the above advice may make a fresh application on form D4, obtainable from a Post Office. Such patients will be invited by DVLA to detail their medical condition and give consent to their doctors and specialists giving reports about their condition. Failure to give such consent will lead to mandatory refusal of the application in accordance with the Road Traffic Act.*

8) *Following the reinstatement of a licence the patient's clinician should be mindful to monitor the patient's mental health and compliance with any pertinent treatment. Medical practitioners must, in accordance with these guidelines, inform DVLA where they know that the patient is not complying with the treatment or their mental state has deteriorated to the point that they are likely to be a source of danger to the public. The General Medical Council ethical code allows such notification where the public are at risk and a patient has failed to fulfil the Road Traffic Act obligation to immediately inform DVLA. It is acknowledged that monitoring patient compliance can sometimes be impracticable.*

9) *It is impossible to frame regulations for drivers with personality disorder (although matters may appear clear cut with psychopathic disorder), but it is likely that those constituting a danger can be identified by a record of police offences, not necessarily connected with driving (such as assault or drunkenness). These can be excluded on a non-medical basis, and can be dealt with without any medical information."*

Notification to the Licensing Centre

The law obliges driving licence holders to notify DVLA as soon as they become aware of any medical condition, including mental disorders, likely to affect their driving. Some mental disorders lead to lack of insight to the point that an individual driver may not be able to fulfil his notification obligation, even though he is a danger to himself and others driving. In these circumstances the doctor should either ensure relatives or friends make a notification on behalf of the sick driver or, in accordance with the General Medical Council ethical code, make a notification directly to the Licensing Agency. Where the patient's affairs are in the hands of a solicitor, the doctor should advise the solicitor to make a formal notification to DVLA.

Advice to Patients

should be advised to immediately stop driving and notify the DVLA, Swansea, in the following circumstances:

1. Where the mental state is seriously unstable or there is significant impairment of concentration or judgement.

2. Where essential medication is likely to impair safe driving.

3. Where the patient is not compliant to essential medicine.

4. In any case where a mental disorder significant to safe driving is expected to last for more than 3 months.

Patients taking psychoactive medications should be particularly warned never to take alcohol before driving.

REFERENCES

Royal College of Psychiatrists (1993) Psychiatric standards of fitness to drive large goods vehicles (LGVs) and passenger carrying vehicles (PCVs), Psychiatric Bulletin, 17, 631–2.

PSYCHIATRIC DISORDERS	GROUP I ENTITLEMENT	GROUP II ENTITLEMENT
NEUROSIS e.g. Anxiety state, Depression	DVLA need not be notified. Driving need not cease. Patients must be warned about the possible effects of medication which may affect fitness. However, serious psychoneurotic episodes affecting or likely to affect driving should be notified to DVLA and the person advised not to drive.	Driving should cease with serious *acute* mental illness from whatever cause. Driving may be permitted when the person is symptom free and stable for a period of 6 months. Medication must not cause side effects which would interfere with alertness or concentration. Driving may be permitted also if the mental illness is long standing but maintained symptom free on small doses of psychotropic medication with no side effects likely to impair driving performance. Psychiatric reports may be required.

MENTAL DISORDERS

PSYCHIATRIC DISORDERS	GROUP I ENTITLEMENT	GROUP II ENTITLEMENT
PSYCHOSIS Schizo-Affective, Acute Psychosis, Schizophrenia	6 months off the road after an acute episode requiring hospital admission. Licence restored after freedom from symptoms during this period, and the person demonstrates that he/she complies safely with recommended medication and shows insight into the condition. 1/2/3 year licence with medical review on renewal. Loss of insight or judgement will lead to recommendation to refuse/revoke.	Recommended refusal or revocation. At least 3 years off driving, during which must be stable and symptom free, and not on major psychotropic or neuroleptic medication, except Lithium. Consultant Psychiatric examination required before restoration of licence, to confirm that there is no residual impairment, the applicant has insight and would be able to recognise if he became unwell. There should be no significant likelihood of recurrence. Any psychotropic medication necessary must be of low dosage and not interfere with alertness or concentration or in any way impair driving performance.
MANIC DEPRESSIVE PSYCHOSIS	6–12 months off the road after an acute episode of hypomania requiring hospital admission, depending upon the severity and frequency of relapses. Licence restored after freedom from symptoms during this period and safe compliance with medication. 1/2/3 year licence with medical review on renewal. Loss of insight or judgement will lead to recommendation to refuse/revoke.	AS ABOVE.

MENTAL DISORDERS

PSYCHIATRIC DISORDERS	GROUP I ENTITLEMENT	GROUP II ENTITLEMENT
DEMENTIA – Organic Brain Disorders e.g. Alzheimer's disease et alia NB: There is no single marker to determine fitness to drive but it is likely that driving may be permitted if there is retention of ability to cope with the general day to day needs of living, together with adequate levels of insight and judgement.	If early dementia, driving may be permitted if there is no significant disorientation in time and space, and there is adequate retention of insight and judgement. Annual medical review required. Likely to be recommended to be refused or revoked if disorientated in time and space, and especially if insight has been lost or judgement is impaired.	Recommended permanent refusal or revocation if the condition is likely to impair driving performance.
SEVERE MENTAL HANDICAP means a state of arrested or incomplete development of mind which includes severe impairment of intelligence and social functioning.	Severe mental handicap is a prescribed disability, licence must be refused or revoked. If stable, mild to moderate mental handicap it may be possible to hold a licence, but he/she will need to demonstrate adequate functional ability at the wheel, and be otherwise stable.	Recommended permanent refusal or revocation if severe. Minor degrees of mental handicap when the condition is stable with no medical or psychiatric complications may be able to have a licence. Will need to demonstrate functional ability at the wheel.
PERSONALITY DISORDER (including post head injury syndrome and psychopathic disorders)	If seriously disturbed such as evidence of violent outbreaks or alcohol abuse and likely to be a source of danger at the wheel, licence would be refused or revoked. Licence restricted after medical reports that behaviour disturbances have been satisfactorily controlled.	Recommended refusal or revocation if associated with serious behaviour disturbance likely to be a source of danger at the wheel. If the person matures and psychiatric reports confirm stability supportive, licence may be permitted/restored. Consultant Psychiatrist report required.

NB: A person holding entitlement to Group I (i.e. motor car/motor bike) or Group II (i.e. LGV/PCV), who has been relicensed following an acute psychotic episode, of whatever type, should be advised as part of follow up that if the condition recurs, driving should cease and DVLA be notified. General guidance with respect to psychotropic/neuroleptic medication is contained under the appropriate section in the text.

Alcohol and illicit drug misuse/dependency are dealt with under their specific sections.

Reference is made in the introductory page to the current GMC guidance to doctors concerning disclosure in the public interest without the consent of the patient.

11

VISION

Principal Author: Greg Munton FRCS FRC Ophth*

INTRODUCTION

It is estimated that something like 95% of the sensory input to the brain required for driving comes from vision. There is little statistical evidence in several large surveys to imply that defects in the various parameters of vision necessary for driving are importantly associated with road accidents or road traffic violations (Burg, 1964,[1] 1965,[2] 1967,[3] 1968:[4] Hills and Burg 1977;[5] Davidson 1985).[6] Johnson and Keltner (1983)[7] reviewed the field losses in 20,000 eyes and showed that drivers with significant field defects had double the average accident rate. Since January 1983, the European Commission has laid down definitive minimum visual standards for driving licence holders in the member states. The relatively weak statistical correlation between road traffic accidents and visual impairments may reflect the reluctance of people with inadequate vision to drive and the previous deselection of visually impaired drivers by the driving test.

Notification to DVLA –
Chapter 2, Part 1 defines the notification requirements.

Visual Acuity

If a person drives a motor vehicle on a road with a visual acuity, with glasses or contact lenses if worn, such that they are unable to read, in good daylight, a registration mark fixed to a motor vehicle containing letters and figures 79.4 millimetres high (3 1/8"), at a distance of 20.5

---

*   *Consultant Ophthalmologist, Kent County Ophthalmic & Aural Hospital, Maidstone, Kent.*

metres (67ft) (except in the case of pedestrian controlled vehicles when the distance is 12.3 metres) (40ft 4), they are guilty of an offence. Section 96 of the 1988 Road Traffic Act allows a constable "having reason to suspect that a person driving a motor vehicle may be guilty of the above offence" to check whether they can comply with the number plate requirement. Also, if a person refuses to submit to the test, they are guilty of an offence. The number plate test is routinely applied at the driving test. Drasdo and Haggerty (1977)[8] Snellen tested persons failing the number plate test at driving test centres and found the mean equivalent to equate to 6/10 Snellen. Notwithstanding its simplicity, the test has served well, since its introduction in 1934 and is in conformity with the European Directive requirement. Belgium and France also enforce driver visual acuity standards through number plate tests. The number plate test is a daylight test of static visual acuity and of glare and contrast sensitivity in a real highway environment. It has the advantage that it can be self-administered at any time or be administered by a police constable. This enables it to be prescribed in law as failure to complete the test satisfactorily is an absolute disability for the driving of motor vehicles. Although the test may seem archaic, it has much relevance to those conditions causing glare in bright light, such as cataract.

The number plate standard is absolute in law and not open to interpretation.

Ocular Disabilities and their effect on driving

VISUAL FIELD DEFECTS

An adequate field of vision is necessary for driving. It is recognised, however, that persons who have only one eye can drive a car safely.

VISION

Monocular vision is not a cause for disqualification from Group I driving, provided the visual field is normal in the remaining eye, and except for a short period to adapt, which might be three months, after the loss of use of one eye. An adequate field of vision (120 degrees) is required by the European Union Directive.* Work in the United States (Council & Allen 1974)[14] indicated that fewer than 1% of drivers had visual fields of less than 120 degrees width, and there is some evidence that these drivers are more prone to accidents; in particular drivers with restricted fields may be prone to a slightly higher incidence of side collision. Johnson & Keltner (1983)[7] reviewed the incidence of field loss in 20,000 eyes and the relationship to driving performance and found patients with significant field loss had twice the average road traffic accident rate.

Binocular field defects such a bitemporal hemianopia, homonymous hemianopia, and homonymous quadrantopia cause difficulty in driving especially if complete to the central fixation point. Any considerable deterioration in the binocular field of vision is a hazardous defect and is a disability which should be notified to DVLA.

The Royal College of Ophthalmologists in its advice to the DVLA has defined The standard of the minimal field of vision for safe driving as "a field of vision of at least 120 degrees on the horizontal measured by the Goldmann perimeter using the III4e settings (or equivalent perimetry). In addition there should be no *significant* defect in the binocular field which encroaches within 20 degrees of fixation above or below the meridian. By these means homonymous or bitemporal defects which come close to fixation whether hemianopic or quadrantopic are not accepted as safe for driving. Isolated scotomata

---

* *This will be incorporated in UK law before July 1996 as an absolute standard.*

represented in the binocular field near to the central fixation point may also be inconsistent with safe driving. The test must monitor the central area as well as its outer perimeter".

This standard is not equipment specific, and permits other equivalent *perimeters* including autoperimeters where the programs are easily specified and not time consuming. The following, (not exclusive) list will satisfy the standard:

a. *Older manual perimeters (Lister etc.) using 3mm targets at 1/3 metre distance.*

b. *The Gultron Biotronics Autofield I and Fieldmaster perimeters using their basic programs.*

c. *The Humphrey Perimeter (3 zone, 61 point program).*

d. *The Dicon Perimeter AP2000 (Target 2500 Asb. Bowl 31.5 Asb).*

e. *The Octopus Perimeter 500EZ (Program No.7).*

f. *The Tubinger TAP2000ct. (Program No.6).*

g. *The Henson Perimeter 4000. (Full field strategy).*

h. *In addition The Esterman Test which can be monocular or binocular can be programmed into perimeters such as the Dicon, Henson and Humphrey and can test 130 degrees field with some enhancement of the binocular field as naturally occurs. While the test can be exactly related to the Goldmann III4e settings it is probably the least stringent test which will satisfy the standard.*

CATARACT AND REFRACTIVE SURGERY

Cataract is an opacity developing in the natural lens. It may be associated with traumatic injury to the eye but most cases develop slowly as part of the ageing process over many years. The condition is invariably associated with bright light glare. In this context, the retroreflective number plate test in good light may be superior to "in office" Snellen visual acuity test charts in assessing driving safety. Approximately 40% of the population over 70 years of age may have some degree of cortical lens opacification. They experience glare when the sun is at a low angle as well as the optical glare round on coming headlights when driving at night. Many self-restrict their night driving and avoid sunrise and sunset driving on this account. Experiments in bright daylight or with bright light glare acuity testers such as the Miller Nadler device, show that whilst 71% of drivers with early cataracts may achieve 6/12, when tested indoors, only 30% can achieve the same level out of doors or under bright glare. (Neumann 1988).[9] 20% were as much as 5 Snellen lines worse in glare. Failure to achieve a satisfactory driving acuity is increasingly being seen as a valid indication for early cataract surgery.

Refractive Procedures such as radial keratotomy (RK) and to a lesser extent excimer laser photorefractive keratoplasty (PRK), for myopia may also be associated with glare problems.

HIGH POWERED GLASSES

Most cataract surgery in the UK is now performed replacing the natural lens by an implanted intra-ocular lens; further correction with spectacles is then relatively minor. Prior to the general installation of intra-ocular lenses during cataract surgery, high powered lenses with an up to 25% magnification were used and could cause significant spherical and chromatic aberration. Similar effects may occur with other high powered spectacles used to correct major refractive errors. These spectacles can result in significant distortion and blurring of

VISION

peripheral vision and a period of adaptation and education in head movements may be helpful. Contact lenses because of their more normal magnification and spatial relationships can readily overcome these problems but some older drivers do not cope well with their management.

STRABISMUS AND DIPLOPIA

Strabismus (squint) does not disbar from driving providing the acuity standard is met and there is no diplopia. Mild degrees of extra-ocular muscle imbalance, such as latent squints, may cause eye strain and ocular fatigue, and can cause blurring or occasional diplopia. These conditions should receive adequate treatment before permitting driving. Prismatic glasses controlling diplopia are acceptable but uncontrolled double vision should be reported to DVLA by the driver. Ordinary driving is generally permitted subject to the driver satisfactorily adapting to driving wearing an eyepatch and giving DVLA an undertaking that it will be worn whenever driving. Diplopia in a very limited direction of gaze may be acceptable and in general a field of binocular single vision 120 degrees wide may be allowed. Stereopsis does not function far beyond the end of the car and there is no evidence that it is necessary for judging the distance from objects or other vehicles in front on the open road, other visual clues to distance and perception being used. Variable diplopia, and ptosis increased by fatigue is common in ocular or myaesthenia gravis and may be controlled by medication so as to allow driving. Episodes of diplopia due to transient ischaemic attacks occur in cerebrovascular lesions; they may be precipitated by changes in head and neck posture. Associated brain stem disturbances may give rise to vertigo and visual obscurations. Severe gaze palsies due to defects of lateral conjugate movement can also make driving very dangerous. Nystagmus is not a bar to driving provided the number plate test can be passed but associated oscillopsia can give rise to fixation problems due to the motion of the vehicle.

MIGRAINE

The majority of migraine sufferers have sufficient prodromal warning of an attack to avoid using a motor vehicle. However, this may be difficult in the case of professionally employed drivers and it is questionable whether severe frequent migraine is compatible with occupational driving. Bright scintillations, fortification figures, patterns or dark obscurations expanding to occupy much of the field of vision may occur whilst driving. The driver normally has to stop and rest until the episode ceases. It is rare for driving licences to be refused on account of migraine but homonymous hemianopic migraine without adequate prodromal warning renders driving very dangerous.

COLOUR VISION

An extensive study of London Bus drivers (Norman 1960)[10] showed no correlation between road traffic accidents and colour defects. The majority of colour blind drivers are able to distinguish traffic lights by their intensity and position and are aware of the relative movement of other traffic. Green direction signs on trunk roads and blue direction signs on motorways do not obscure their intrinsic message for colour defective drivers as they rely on contrast. Gross loss or sensitivity at the red end of the spectrum could pose problems where single red lights are used to mark hazards.

LOW LUMINANCE MYOPIA

Less than 7% of drivers have true low luminance myopia, a very small myopic change over their normal refractive state in bright light. (Epstein & Tengroth).[11] However the law properly requires us to drive by at least dipped headlamps in the dark, a condition which creates road luminance between the lower range of photopic (daylight) vision and the upper range of mesopic (twilight) vision, that is above the scotopic range where low luminance myopia usually occurs. Where a driver has a small added myopic correction for countryside night driving he may be disadvantaged by over myopic correction in city lights. Under poor luminance visual function is depressed by factors, such as dilation of the pupil, reduced retinal discrimination, and even night hypermetropia in a few cases. (VIV IV, Chauhan & Charman).[12] In all cases contrast sensitivity and visual acuity are quite reduced when dark adapted, even if wearing full optical correction.

DARK ADAPTATION

Failure of dark adaptation is rare in the healthy eye though more serious faults in dark adaptation occur in retinitis pigmentosa, congenital stationary night blindness, advanced choroido-retinitis, and after extensive pan retinal photocoagulation. In these circumstances visual acuity and visual fields are severely restricted in reduced luminance. These persons should declare their condition to DVLA Because of progression of the disease few drivers with retinitis pigmentosa are able to retain their driving licence far into adult life.

LASER TREATMENT FOR DIABETIC RETINOPATHY

Treatment of proliferative (diabetic) retinopathy by laser ablation (pan retinal photocoagulation) of the mid peripheral retina can cause reduced visual field and reduced acuity particularly under dark conditions, sufficient to jeopardise the right to drive. (Williamson, 1991).[13] While

VISION

failure to treat proliferation adequately leads to almost certain blindness, warning of the possible risk to the right to drive properly forms part of informed consent on commencing treatment. If patients fail to meet the required visual field standards above they must report their condition to DVLA.

GROUP II DRIVERS

Department of Transport published statistics show that large goods vehicles have approximately 3 times the road traffic accident fatality rate per mile travelled compared with cars. Passenger carrying vehicles have up to four times the fatality rate of cars. European Council directives therefore apply specifically higher visual acuity standards to Group II drivers.

a. A new UK acuity standard will come into force on or before 1 July 1996 and will apply to all new applicants (see Chapter 2) and require:

   i. at least 6/9 in the better eye

   ii. at least 6/12 in the other eye

   iii. an uncorrected visual acuity of at least 3/60 in each eye tested separately. (3/60 = reading 6/60 line at 3 metres from the chart.)

Failure to satisfy any one of the above clauses i, ii or iii, disbars.

b. The uncorrected standard above precludes cataract surgery cases unless (a) above can be met.

c. Contact lenses are permitted if the standards are met including the unaided standard of 3/60ths in each eye separately.

d. Any optical correction must be tolerated.

e. Diplopia, if uncontrolled disbars as does wearing an eyepatch.

f. Any significant field defect disbars. New drivers and drivers on renewal will be required to meet this as a substantive standard as part of the second EU Driving Licence Directive.

ADVICE TO PATIENTS

It is wise to encourage drivers to test themselves regularly to the number plate standard i.e. reading a number plate fixed to a vehicle, in good daylight, with glasses or contact lenses if worn at a distance of 20.5 metres (67 feet) in the case of a number plate 79.4 millimetres (3 1/8 inches) high. **In the case of failure to meet the standard, drivers must notify DVLA immediately and stop driving otherwise they are committing a criminal offence.**

Drivers requiring an optical correction to meet the number plate standard must be advised to wear their spectacles or contact lenses whenever driving and are legally required to do so. In either case, it is advisable to carry a spare pair of glasses (this is mandatory when driving in some European Union States).

Thick spectacle frames and those with deep side pieces such as library glasses may obscure vision and should be avoided for driving.

One eyed drivers and who have an adequate field of vision are permitted to drive Group I but not buses and lorries (Group II). A period of adaptation is required after the loss of one eye function – usually three months may be necessary to drive safety. An ophthalmological opinion is advisable.

There is no truth in the statement that tinted lenses and windscreens increase driving safety by reducing glare at night. All of these reduce visibility and contrast sensitivity and increase glare recovery time. Drivers with limited visual acuity and those with cataracts should avoid selecting vehicles with tinted windows and tinted lenses should be avoided when night driving. Neutral tinted, polarising and light range photo-chromic lenses may be useful when driving in the glare of bright sunlight, especially for those with an early cataract. However, polarising lenses can conceal surface road water and reveal strain patterns in toughened windscreens. The earlier and now obsolete photo-chromic lenses had a slow lightening phase which is hazardous on entering road tunnels etc. Drivers who have had cataract surgery with intra-ocular lenses or contact lenses should generally wait until adaptation before resuming driving. Bilateral cataract patients who have not been provided with intra-ocular lenses and others who also require high power glasses should be encouraged to try to tolerate contact lenses. High powered spectacles cause considerable blurring of peripheral vision as well as blind spots and need a period of adaptation.

Drivers normally wearing contact lenses who have to revert to spectacles may need a period of adaptation to the altered image size in the case of myopia – it can take several hours, or days.

Any ocular disease or other factor which leads to failure to meet the visual acuity standard of the number plate test or results bilateral in visual field defects, or insuperable double vision or dark adaptation defects should be reported immediately to the Driver and Vehicle Licensing Agency, and the motor insurer. Progressive visual disabilities and diseases, particularly when affecting both eyes must be reported, in particular, progressive myopia, macula degeneration, cataract, glaucoma, and significant bilateral field defects. Uveitis and keratitis should be reported if affecting both eyes.

REFERENCES

1. Burg A (1964) An investigation of some relationships between dynamic visual acuity, static visual acuity and driving record. Report No. 64–18. Los Angeles: University of California, Department of Engineering.

2. Burg A (1965) Apparatus for measurement of dynamic visual acuity. Perceptual and Motor Skills, 20. 231–234.

3. Burg A (1967) The relationship between vision test scores and driving record: General findings. Report No. 67–24. Los Angeles: University of California, Department of Engineering.

4. Burg A (1968) Vision test scores and driving record: Additional findings. Report No. 68–27. Los Angeles: University of California, Department of Engineering.

5. Hills RL and Burg A (1977) A reanalysis of Californian driver vision data: general findings. Research Report LR 768, Transport and Road Research Laboratory, Crowthorne.

6. Davison P A (1985) Inter-relationships between British drivers' visual disabilities, age and road accident histories. Oph. Physiol. Optics. 5: 195–204.

7. Johnson CA and Keltner JL (1983) Incidence of visual field losses in 20,000 eyes and its relationship to driving performance. Arch opthalmol 101, 371–375.

8. Drasdo M and Haggarty CM (1977) A Comparison of British number plates and Snellen vision tests for Car Driving. Research Report RF 676, Transport and Road Research Laboratory, Crowthorne.

9. Neuman AC, McCary SR, Steedle TO, Sanders DR, Raanan MG (1988) The relationship between indoor and outdoor Snellen visual acuity in cataract patients. J Cataract & Implant Surgery, 14: 35–39.

10. Norman LG (1960) Medical aspects of road safety. Lancet 1, 989–994.

11. Epstein D Ingelstam E, Jansson K, Tengroth B (1981) Low luminance myopia as measured with a laser optometer. Acta Ophthalmologica 59, 928–943.

12. Chauhan K, Charman W N (1993) Changes in Refractive Error under Night-time Driving Conditions. Vision in Vehicles – IV Gale AG et al, (Editors) North Holland, Amsterdam. 35–44.

13. Williamson TH, George N, Flanagan DW, Norris V, Blamires T (1991) Driving standards visual fields in diabetic patients after pan retinal laser photocoagulation. Vision in Vehicles – III, Gale AG et al (Editors) North Holland Amsterdam. 265–272.

14. Council FM & Allen JA (1974) A study of the visual fields of North Carolina drivers and their relationship to accidents. University of North Carolina, Highway and Safety Research Centre, North Carolina.

VISION

VISUAL DISORDERS	GROUP I ENTITLEMENT	GROUP II ENTITLEMENT
VISUAL ACUITY	Must be able to meet the above requirement. (In practice this corresponds to between 6/9 and 6/12 on the Snellen chart).	Applicants will be barred in law* if the visual acuity using corrective lenses if necessary is worse than 6/9 in the better or 6/12 in the other eye or the uncorrected acuity in each eye separately is worse than 3/60. See Chapter 2 about grandfather rights.
MONOCULAR VISION	Need not notify DVLA if able to meet the visual acuity standard _and_ has adapted to the disability.	Not permitted* but see Chapter 2, Part 1 about grandfather rights.
VISUAL FIELD DEFECTS e.g. homonymous, hemianopia and homonymous quadrantanopia, severe bilateral glaucoma, severe bilateral cataract, failed bilateral cataract extraction, severe bilateral retinopathy (diabetes, retinitis pigmentosa) and other serious bilateral eye disorders.	Driving must cease unless confirmed able to meet recommended national guideline for visual field, _see previous paragraph on visual field defects._	Recommended permanent refusal or revocation if associated with pathological field defects. Normal binocular vision is required for entitlement to drive these vehicles.
DIPLOPIA	Cease driving on diagnosis. May resume driving on confirmation to the Licensing Authority that it is controlled by glasses or a patch which he undertakes to wear while driving.	Recommended permanent refusal or revocation if insuperable diplopia.

VISUAL DISORDERS	GROUP I ENTITLEMENT	GROUP II ENTITLEMENT
NIGHT BLINDNESS	Cease driving if unable to satisfy visual acuity and visual field requirements at all times.	Driving not permitted unless able to fully meet the Group II eyesight requirements.
COLOUR BLINDNESS	Need not notify DVLA. Driving may continue with no restriction on licence.	Need not notify DVLA; as for Group I.

*   Requirements effective from July 1996 for all applicants and new applicants.

12

PRESCRIBED MEDICINES AND DRIVING

Principal Author: Dr John Taylor CBE FRCP FFOM*

Many drugs can impair driving ability. Everest et al 1989[1] reported on a Transport Research Laboratory project analysing drugs found in the body fluids of 1273 road traffic accident fatality victims. Analyses both quantitative and qualitative were undertaken at the London National Poisons Unit. Overall, 7.4% of persons killed in road accidents showed the presence of drugs likely to affect the central nervous system whilst alcohol was detected in 35%. Cannabis was present in 2.6% of the victims, however, this needs to be considered against a figure of over 20% cannabinoids found, about the same time, in outpatient attendees at the Homerton Hospital, London. There was a greater incidence of psycho-active drugs in the age group 60+. Tricyclic anti-depressants were present in three (0.2%), one a driver, one a motorcyclist and one a pedestrian who also had alcohol detected. Benzodiazepines were detected in 1.9% of which 6 were passengers. Prominent amongst psycho-active medicaments associated with fatality were the presence of anti-convulsants which appeared to be present in larger numbers than the prevalence of epilepsy in the community would suggest. These fatalities probably related to epilepsy rather than the treatments for epilepsy.

Cimbura et al (1982)[2] analysed the body fluids of 401 drivers and 83 pedestrians in Ontario killed in road traffic accidents. 57% had detectable alcohol present and 9.5% had psychoactive substances in their body fluids of which diazepam accounted for 67.5%. 13 of the 15 cases with cannabinoids were found to have alcohol in addition.

---

*   *Chairman Transport Committee, Medical Commission on Accident Prevention.*

Vine et al (1982)[3] analysed the blood of 425 road traffic accident fatalities in Sydney. Cannabinoids were excluded because they could not be detected in haemolised blood. Diazepam was present in 13, anti-epileptics in 7 and alcohol in 51%.

Graham Smith (1979–1981)[4] studied the drugs in the body fluids of 707 drivers and motor cyclists involved in road traffic accidents and admitted to Oxford hospitals. The study involved just short of a 1/3 of such casualties. 18% had detectable alcohol present; 5.7% had benzodiazepines detected and 1.6% had tricyclic antidepressants detected. Women had twice the involvement of men up to the age of 55 whilst after that age, there is no sex incidence difference.

Skegg et al (1979)[5] reviewed the prescribing of benzodiazepines and driving accidents. This study was possible because 13 general practices in the Oxford University practice area had on-line data linkage. The study reviewed the prescriptions and clinical notes from these practices compared with 1425 matched controls. In the study, 57 people were involved in road traffic accidents, 21 in cars, 22 in motor cycles and 14 cyclists. 6 of the road traffic accident victims (10.5%) had taken sedatives and tranquillisers against 36 controls (2.5%). Statistically those taking tranquillisers had five times the road traffic accident risk of those not taking them. However, these results need to be considered with caution as overall only 6 road traffic accident victims had actually taken tranquillisers and sedatives.

Detection of a substance does not imply that it caused the road traffic accident.

Ethyl alcohol, the most frequently taken drug can seriously potentiate psychotropic medicines. Prescribers need to take care also in case poly pharmacy results in detrimental interactions between medicines causing driver fitness impairment.

PRESCRIBED MEDICINES
AND DRIVING

Something like 50 new ethical products are launched onto the British market every year. It often takes some years before a new product's metabolism is fully comprehended. Unlike alcohol, serum levels often bear little relationship to observable effects. Studies have clearly demonstrated a mean increase in road traffic accident involvement as blood alcohol concentrations increase over 80mg per 100ml. Some drugs improve driving performance, as for example non-steroidal anti-inflammatory drugs in the case of drivers with arthritis or modest doses of betablockers or tranquillisers in the case of persons suffering from panic attacks. Specific warnings in relation to an effect on driving on the packaging, labelling of medicines or in an information leaflet in a form that it is understandable by the patient is now compulsory following EU Council Directive 92/27 EEC and the 1992 Medicines (Labelling) Amendment Regulations (Statutory Instruments 1992 No.3273 and 3274). However, there is no formal requirement in British or EU legislation for the safety of psychotropic medications to be specifically tested in regard to their effect on driving. Clinical trials do not usually consider that aspect. Some University departments and the Transport Research Laboratory undertake specific fitness to drive assessments of medicinal products on behalf of some pharmaceutical manufacturers, usually when they particularly wish to prove the non-impairing efficacy of a product to promote sales. It is important that such assessment should involve not only healthy volunteers but also those suffering from the condition for which the medicament is intended to treat.

Prescribing policy by practitioners in the United Kingdom has in recent years tended to address carefully the road safety issue. Amphetamine prescribing other than for narcolepsy, barbiturate prescribing other than in epilepsy and a significant and substantial reduction in the general prescribing of long and medium acting benzodiazepines has occurred. Other improvements are the prescribing of antihistamines that virtually don't cross the blood brain barrier. There is considerable individual variation between individuals and their levels of psychotropic impairment relating to a specific medicine. It is important that any prescribed drugs likely to impair driving performance should be given on a trial basis for at least a week telling the patient not to drive in the meantime.

Misuse of prescribed medicines by those other than for whom the prescription was intended is becoming more frequent. Patients tend to hoard prescribed drugs and many elderly patients accumulate considerable quantities of potentially hazardous medicines in their homes. These are available to be stolen and then may appear as street sales.

It is important to urge patients to destroy any unused medicines or return them to pharmacist. Examples of prescribed medicament misuse are a 20 year old driving licence applicant who had purchased some pills in a public house and whose urine showed excessive levels of a drug used exclusively for the treatment of Parkinson's disease. In another, an ambulance attendant wanted to become an ambulance driver and was found to have cocaine and diamorphine on urinalysis, he later confessed to requiring all patients that he conveyed to a local hospice for terminal care to hand over all their medicines to him.

Sleeping tablets of long and medium action present a particular driver safety problem. A suitable hypnotic, universally safe for drivers has yet to be invented. In the past there have been many contenders including thalidomide. It is best to avoid prescribing nitrazepam to drivers as in some individuals its maximum blood effect is reached only after they wake up in the morning. Temazepam has been carefully researched by the Institute of Aviation Medicine in regard to airline pilots. It has a

PRESCRIBED MEDICINES
AND DRIVING

four hour effective life. Pilots are permitted to take it in a dose of 10–20mg, taken *only occasionally* and *at least twelve hours before flying.* Prescription of temazepam gel filled capsules should be avoided as they have particularly been subject to abuse and gangrene has followed their injection.

Legal Aspects of Drugs and Driving

Section 4 of 1988 Road Traffic Act states:

"A person who, when driving or attempting to drive a motor vehicle on a road or other public place is unfit to drive through drink or drugs is guilty of an offence." A similar offence relates to a person who is "in charge of a motor vehicle which is on a road or other public place".

The law shows no distinction between the person who is unfit through drugs taken in the prescribed dosage on the advice of a medical or nursing practitioner and those misused. Thus the Appeal Court has ruled that a person unfit to drive by insulin, is guilty of a section 4 offence. Civil law claims of negligence have been made against medical practitioners who have prescribed drugs to individuals who have subsequently claimed that they were not fully and correctly informed as to the possible affects of the medicine. The Medical Defence Associations urge practitioners to ensure that a patient who is a driver and who is prescribed a potentially dangerous psycho-active substance should be fully informed concerning the risk when driving.

Continuing drug misuse and dependency are disabilities which must be reported to DVLA by drivers and applicants for a driving licence.

Drug/Driving Impairment Studies

Advances in therapeutics and a greater understanding of drug action in

PRESCRIBED MEDICINES
AND DRIVING

man have made a logical approach possible to ensure that a particular therapy does not impair driving performance. Substantial work has been undertaken by the Institute of Aviation Medicine who have evolved a list of medicines safe for pilots.[6-11] Over the last 10 years, the Department of Transport's Transport and Road Research Laboratory has designed a battery of sensitive tests to measure driving impairment by drugs as compared with measured doses of alcohol.[12] Similar studies have been undertaken by some University departments. *At the time of writing there is no statutory compulsion either national or international requiring psychotropic drugs possibly affecting the driving task to be specifically assessed.* A large number of testing procedures have to be included in these assessments from simple pencil and paper tests, reaction times, critical flicker fusion, the EEG recordings, hazard perception simulators and off and on the road track testing. Dose time response data relating impaired performance to the whole of the therapeutic dose range of the medicine is essential. Car accidents are seldom related to loss of control and it may be far more important to study the decision making process of whether a specific manoeuvre is thought to be possible than the ability to carry out accurately the manoeuvre itself. Equally important is to study the ability to cope with unexpected situations rather than the skill involved in negotiating stationary obstacles.

Advice to Patients

It is important to assume that the majority of adult patients are either actual or potential motor vehicle drivers and to tailor prescribing to avoid impairing medicines. Pedestrian caused accidents are an increasing problem particularly amongst the over 60 age group and can result from injudicious prescribing.

PRESCRIBED MEDICINES
AND DRIVING

Suggestions for advice to patients to taking CNS active drugs.

1. Do not exceed the stated dose.

2. Do not drive until the nature and extent of the side effects or the main effect are known.

3. Do not take any other medicines or drugs during treatment unless they are prescribed for you and *avoid drinking alcohol before driving.*

4. Stimulant and euphoria producing drugs may lead to unnecessary risks being taken.

5. Never drive if feeling unwell and stop driving if feeling unwell in the course of a journey.

6. Avoid driving within 24 hours of a general anaesthetic unless the anaesthetist says you can.

7. Psychoactive antihistamines can be dangerous when taken for motion sickness on a short sea crossing. Hyoscine is safer but is best avoided in the age 70 plus group.

8. Driving, or being in charge, when under the influence of a drug is an offence under Section 4 of the Road Traffic Act 1988, conviction carries an automatic penalty of disqualification from driving.

Group II Drivers: Strict criteria have to be applied in the case of professional drivers including emergency and taxi vehicle drivers. Often where long term medication is required, frequently the underlying medical condition precludes the holding of a Group II licence. The chapters in this book dealing with the various conditions should be consulted where appropriate. Something like one third of Group II drivers undertake shift work. Others have to spend nights away from home which may not be conducive to a good night's sleep. In general, Group II driving is not recommended where a medicament has to be prescribed which is likely to impair driving ability. Long distance drivers may be affected by potentially lethal sleepiness at the wheel. Sleeping tablets wherever possible should be avoided, but it is recognised that due to the rotation of duties a short acting hypnotic such as temazepam tablets (not capsules) may be necessary on the understanding that it is <u>not</u> taken within 12 hours of driving or in a dose exceeding 20mg and that it will be taken <u>periodically</u>, say not more than once or twice a week.

REFERENCES

1. Everest J.T., Tunbridge R.J and Widdop B. 1989. The incidence of drugs in road accident fatalities. TRL Research Report 202 Transport Research Laboratory, Crowthorne, Berkshire RG11 6AU, England.

2. Cimbura G, Lucas D.M., Bennett R.C., Warren R.A. and Simpson H.M. 1982. Incidence and toxicological aspects of drugs detected in 484 fatally injured drivers and pedestrians in Ontario. Journal of Forensic Sciences 27, 855–867.

3. Vine J.H. and Watson T.R. (1982). The incidence of drugs and alcohol in road traffic accident victims. PP 1–37 University of Sydney, Department of Pharmacy, Sydney.

4. Oxford Road Accident Group. Final Report of Pharmacological team to Transport Research Laboratory. Jan 1982 (unpublished).

5. Skegg D.G.G., Richards S.M. and Doll R (1979). Minor tranquillisers and road accidents British Medical Journal 1, 917–919.

6. Nicholson AN. Antihistamines and sedation. Lancet 1983; ii: 211–12.

7. Currie D, Lewis RV, McDevitt DG, Nicholson AN & Wright NA.
    Central effects of beta-adrenoreceptor antagonists. I: Performance
    and subjective assessments of mood. Br J Clin Pharmacol 1988;
    26:121–8.

8. Currie D, Lewis RV, McDevitt DG, Nicholson AN & Wright NA.
    Central effects of the angiotensin-converting enzyme inhibitor,
    captropril. I: Performance and subjective assessments of mood.
    Br J Clin Pharmacol 1990; 30:527–36.

9. McDevitt DG, Currie D, Nicholson AN & Wright NA & Zetlein MB.
    Central effects of the calcium antagonist, nifedipine. Br J Clin
    Pharmacol 1991; 32:541–9.

10. Nicholson AN. Performance studies with diazepam and its
    hydroxylated metabolites. Br J Clin Pharmacol 1979; 8:39–42S.

11. Nicholson AN & Stone BM. The H2-antagonists, cimetidine and
    ranitidine: Studies on performance. Eur J Clin Pharmacol 1984;
    26:579–82.

12. Irving A & Jones W. Driving impairments due to medicinal drugs:
    Testing methodology. Eur J Clin Pharmacol 1992; 43–61–6.

13

ILLICIT DRUGS AND DRIVING

Principal Authors: Dr Ian Albery BSc Phd*
and Professor John Strang MBBS FRCPsych*

Introduction

The overall prevalence of use of illicit drugs in the UK has increased considerably in recent years. Whilst data are not available from repeat surveys of high school students or from repeat household surveys, such as are available in the United States (e.g. Johnson et al 1990; National Institute on Drug Abuse 1990), some indications of the extent of this increased drug use can be seen from examination of drug arrests. Seizures of illicit drugs by police and customs in the UK increased from 20,000 per annum in 1982 to 70,000 in 1992. The magnitude of this change is all the more extraordinary when it is borne in mind that, over this period, both customs and police have been encouraged to concentrate their efforts on intercepting suppliers, and that many police officers have moved to an approach of informal cautioning for possession of small amounts.

The potential for both illicit and medicinal drugs to affect driving ability, to increase accident likelihood and to put other members of the driving population at an assumed higher risk is highlighted by the enactment of the Road Traffic Act (1988). One clause in the act makes it an offence to drive or attempt to drive any motor vehicle while being unfit through alcohol or drugs. The legislation, therefore, presumes there to be a problem in the ability of the individual to drive after consuming drugs, either licit or illicit.

This chapter considers briefly evidence for the influence of illicit drugs

*   *Addiction Research Unit, National Centre, Institute of Psychiatry,*
    University of London, $ Windsor Walk, London SE5 8AF.

ILLICIT DRUGS AND DRIVING

(e.g. heroin, cocaine, cannabis) on driving performance, and also the effects of pharmacological drugs prescribed for dependence (e.g. methadone) on such skills. The discussion will focus primarily on three drug types; cannabis/marijuana, opiates and stimulants.

Cannabis/marijuana

Cannabis remains the most frequently seized illicit drug, and still accounts for more than three-quarters of all drug seizures in the UK. Furthermore, cannabis itself is not a constant product. The appearance in the mid 1990s of blackmarket cannabis with a much higher concentration of delta-nine-cannabinol is likely to be associated with greater impairment unless drug users are sufficiently knowledgeable and skilful in their use of the drug to reduce the quantity consumed. Epidemiological evidence shows cannabis/marijuana to be the most common illicit drug found in fatally and non-fatally injured drivers (Terhune, 1983; Stoduto et al, 1993; Gjerde et al, 1993, Everest et al 1989), in drivers stopped randomly at checkpoints for voluntary blood analysis (Glauz and Blackburn, 1975) and among drivers arrested for driving while impaired (Brookoff et al, 1994). Experimental studies consistently show the impairing effects of cannabis/marijuana on a number of driving related skills including co-ordination, visual perception, tracking, vigilance, and also in simulated and closed course driving tasks (Moskowitz, 1985; Smiley, 1986).

Opiates

Seizures of heroin steadily increased through to the mid-nineteen eighties and have plateaued, even though the numbers of notifications of opiate addicts have continued to rise by approximately 20% per annum to a 1993 total of 28,000. Although not the most prevalent of illicit drugs found in the blood of drivers killed in accidents, reports consistently show evidence of opiate use prior to accident involvement (Budd et al, 1989; Polkis et al, 1987). Empirical research has focused on the impairing effects of different opiates for addicts and ex-addicts. Results have shown little impairment on many driving related skills (Chesher, 1989) for these groups of users. No evidence exists on the relationship between opiate use and driving performance among novice drug users and non-tolerant individuals. Moreover, research has failed to examine impairment among individuals experiencing withdrawal type symptomology.

A limited number of studies have examined the effects of different routes of administration of opiates on relevant driving skills (Bauer and Pearson, 1956; Fraser et al, 1963). Intravenous use, subcutaneous or intramuscular injection and oral administration have not been shown to be differentially impairing. Recently "chasing the dragon" (inhaling a trail of smoke from the heated drug) has become the main route of heroin use in several parts of the UK with virtually all initiations into heroin use since 1988 being by this new route (Strang et al, 1992). However, no data have yet been gathered which allow assessment of the different implications of this new route of use on driving competence. Heroin use by snorting or 'chasing the dragon' will not only result in different bio-availability (Mo and Way 1966; Huizer, 1983), but also in different pharmaco-kinetics. In this way the relationship between an episode of drug use and any impairment of motor co-ordination will depend not only on the dose of drug administered, but also on the timing of the behaviour i.e. whether the behaviour is being influenced by the initial intoxicating effect of the drug (hence substantially different for the different routes) or the later plateau phase of drug effect (probably similar for the different routes once dose has been corrected).

ILLICIT DRUGS AND DRIVING

Stimulants

Cocaine seizures have increased steadily since the mid-nineteen eighties. However, despite the greater media attention to cocaine seizures, it is the amphetamines which are the stimulant drug more commonly seized in police arrests, with the figure for amphetamine seizures having risen from less than 2,000 in 1982 to more than 10,000 in 1992, thus making it the most common seized illicit drug after cannabis. Seizures of LSD and Ecstasy (and similar psycho-active stimulant drugs) have also increased markedly since the end of the eighties. Statistics from fatal and injury road accidents have found stimulants to be not uncommon among blood analyses (Fortenberry et al, 1986; Ferrara et al, 1991 Vingilis et al, 1993). The experimental study of the impairing effects of stimulants on driving performance have shown that low doses of stimulant ingestion produce little impairment on skills such as divided attention, information processing and vigilance tasks (Hirst, 1987; Burns 1993), although research which utilises higher stimulant doses have demonstrated a positive relationship with impairment and during the withdrawal phase (Ellinwood and Nikaido, 1987).

Interwoven with the spread of cocaine in the UK (Strang et al 1993) new methods of self-administering this cocaine have appeared and become widespread in several parts of the UK. For instance, new routes of freebasing cocaine and the more widespread emergence of smoking cocaine in the form of crack have been identified. No research to date has examined differences in impairment across route of administration.

Mood enhancement and euphoric cognitive states induced by the consumption of stimulants and realised in perceptions of over-confidence, grandiosity and increased risk taking thresholds may be expected to affect driving behaviour. Indeed it is not implausible to

---

145

suggest that increased risk taking in drivers (e.g. increased speed, decreases in tail-gating distance) may result from stimulant consumption (Siegel, 1987).

Benzodiazepines

Although data are not available from police seizures because benzo-diazepine use is not illicit, evidence exists to suggest that non-prescribed use is becoming more widespread (Perera et al, 1987). More recently intravenous benzodiazepine abuse has emerged as a new form of drug abuse (so far almost exclusively restricted to the UK) (Strang, Seivewright and Farrell 1992). One study showed that a half of heroin addicts seeking treatment had also injected benzodiazepines intravenously (Strang et al 1994). Laboratory examination of the relationship between benzo-diazepine use and driving skills and performance do not show consistent impairing effects (Friedel and Staak, 1992), although studies have regularly found traces of benzodiazepines in the bloods of accident involved fatal and non-fatally injured drivers (e.g. Honkanen et al, 1980, Gjerde et al, 1988). Furthermore, the different route of self-administration and higher dose levels of much of the intravenous benzodiazepine abuse described above should prompt carefully consideration as to whether the data currently available (on oral use) can be generalised.

Treatment implications

Treatments which are administered to the drug addict will have an impact on driving competence. Treatments which involve withdrawal off all drugs may involve periods of impairment during phases characterised by acute and protracted withdrawal symptoms. Evidence assessing the impact of withdrawal experience is limited to the study of cocaine where impairment has been observed (Ellinwood and Nikaido,

ILLICIT DRUGS AND DRIVING

1987). Withdrawal from opiates and other drugs of abuse has not been the focus of study for researchers assessing factors involved in driving behaviour and performance.

An extensive literature now exists on oral methadone maintenance programmes in the treatment of heroin addiction (e.g. Ward et al, 1992, Farrell et al, 1994), including specific study of the impact on driving competence. Findings have shown that individuals stabilised on oral methadone demonstrate little impairment on tests of visual acuity and search, peripheral vision, divided attention and vehicle tracking tasks (Moskowitz and Robinson, 1985; Robinson and Moskowitz, 1985). However, it remains unclear how these North American data should be interpreted in the UK where tight monitoring of compliance and supervision of drug consumption are rare features in UK methadone prescribing, with the result that the potential for abuse of the service (and hence greater compromise of co-ordination) would appear to be greater. Other data have found patients on methadone to display impaired driving performance (Berghaus et al, 1993), although it is not evident whether such subjects are maintained individuals or undergoing methadone detoxification.

New drugs currently in development and clinical study offer the promise of more effective stabilisation of the opiate addict in a maintenance substitution programme with less scope for abuse. For instance, buprenorphine (Temgesic) and LAAM (Levo-Alpha-Acetylmethadol) are being studied in the US for the 48 hour cover they purport to deliver from a single dose administered to a patient attending a maintenance programme (Tennant et al, 1986; Fudala et al, 1990). At present LAAM is not yet available in the UK, whilst poorly controlled prescribing of buprenorphine sub-lingual tablets has enabled extensive intravenous abuse of the drug (Sakol, Stark and Sykes, 1989,

Hammersley, Lavell and Forsyth, 1990), and also less extensive buprenorphine abuse by snorting (Strang, 1991).

Special consideration is also required for the impact of prescribed intravenously administered drugs, itself an almost exclusively British treatment practice (Strang et al, 1994). There are approximately 200 heroin addicts who receive prescribed supplies of heroin ampoules for intravenous or intramuscular self-administration (usually taken intravenously). In addition, whilst data on the size of the practice are not publicly available, there are probably several thousand opiate addicts who receive prescribed supplies of methadone ampoules (a form of drug which is not generally available in any other country), with disturbing informal indications that this form of prescribing is becoming increasingly widespread but with little increase in monitoring of compliance. Whilst the overall impact of this parenterally-administered drug may perhaps be similar to the effects from oral administration (so that the US studies can be considered relevant to UK consideration), the impact of these prescribed supplies of heroin or methadone in the period immediately following intravenous self-administration is likely to differ greatly and requires separate consideration.

Suggestions for advice to patients

The doctor is often faced with the need to reconcile different responsibilities; in this instance responsibilities to the individual patient and responsibilities to broader society. First and foremost, the attending doctor has a responsibility to provide care to his/her patient, and to provide this care in the context of the confidential relationship which exists between doctor and patient. Furthermore, if this confidentiality is not seen to exist, then the effect may merely be the continuation of concealment of a drug problem requiring treatment amongst drug users who drive motor vehicles (Strang 1984). Thus confidentiality must not only exist but must be seen to exist.

The doctor should provide information to the patient on the dangers of combining drug use and driving. There is a danger of impairment through abnormal mental states, such as the psychosis scene with higher doses of stimulant drugs (e.g. amphetamines and cocaine), the intoxication of drugs such as the sedative barbiturates and benzodiazepines and the opiates, as well as impairment which may exist during states of drug withdrawal. The drug-using patient may be insufficiently aware of the possibility of impairment of their co-ordination which may occur without subjective awareness (Leirer, Yesavage and Morrow, 1991).

The doctor should discuss with the patient the subject of driving whilst still using drugs or in a state of drug withdrawal. The patient should be reminded of their responsibility to notify the Driver and Vehicle Licensing Authority of any such change in their fitness to drive, and the patient must also be helped to give proper consideration to decisions about driving whilst undergoing such treatment as is prescribed.

Conclusions

The extent of use of illicit drugs in the UK has increased greatly in recent years, and, whilst specific data are not yet available, the extent of overlap between such drug use and driving behaviour is now more widespread. Different drugs are impairing to different degrees, and this is further complicated by the diversity of routes of self-administration of these drugs. Legal status is a poor indicator of the extent of impairment of driving competence. In their confidential consultations with drug-abusing patients, doctors should inform their patients of the dangers of combining drug use and driving, and should encourage the patient to cease driving or alter their driving behaviour whilst drug use continues and treatment is being provided.

REFERENCES

Bauer RO, Pearson RG. The effects of morphine-nalorphine mixtures on psychomotor performance. Journal of Pharmacology and Experimental Therapeutics 1956; 117: 258–264.

Berghaus G, Staak M, Glazinski R, Hoher K, Joo S, Friedel B. Complementary empirical study on the driver fitness of methadone substitution patients. In: Utzelmann H-D, Berghaus G, Kroj, G, eds. Alcohol, Drugs and Traffic Safety. Cologne: Verlag TUV Rheinland, 1993: 120–126.

Burns M (1993). Cocaine effects on performance. In: Utzelmann H-D, Berghaus G, Kroj G, eds. Alcohol, Drugs and Traffic Safety. Cologne: Verlag TUV Rheinland, 1993: 612–613.

Chester GB. Understanding the opioid analgesics and their effects on skills performance. Alcohol, Drugs and Driving 1989; 5:111–138.

Ellinwood EH, Nikaido AM. Stimulant induced impairment: A perspective across dose and duration of use. Alcohol, Drugs and Driving 1987; 3: 19–24.

Everest JT, Tunbridge RJ and Widdop B. 1989. The incidence of drugs in road accident fatalities. TRL Research Report 202 Transport Research Laboratory, Crowthorne, Berkshire RG11 6AU, England.

Farrell M, Ward J, Mattick R, Hall W, Stimson GV, des Jarlais D, Gossop M, Strang J. Methadone maintenance treatment in opiate dependence. A review. British Medical Journal 1994; 309: 997–1001.

Ferrara SD, Zancaner S, Snenghi R, Berto F. Psychoactive drugs involvement in traffic accidents in Italy. In: Perrine, MW eds. Alcohol, Drugs and Traffic Safety. Chicago: National Safety Council, 1991: 260–264.

Fortenberry JS, Brown DB, Shelvin LT. Analysis of drug involvement in traffic accidents. American Journal of Drug and Alcohol Abuse 1986; 12: 257–267.

Fraser HF, Jones BE, Rosenberg DE, Thompson HK. Effects of addiction to intravenous heroin on patterns of physical activity in man. Clinical Pharmacology and Therapeutics 1963; 4: 188–196.

Friedel B, Staak M. Benzodiazepines and driving. Reviews in Contemporary Pharmacotherapy 1992; 3:415–474.

Fudala PJ, Jaffe JH, Dax EM, Johnson RE. Use of buprenorphine in the treatment of opioid addiction. II. Physiologic and behavioural effects of daily and alternate-day administration and abrupt withdrawal. Clinical Pharmacology and Therapeutics 1990;?: 525–534.

Gjerde H, Bjorneboe GE, Bugge A, Drevon DA, Morland J. A three year prospective study of rearrests for driving under influence of alcohol or drugs. Accident Analysis and Prevention 1988; 20:53–57.

Gjerde H, Beylich K-M, Morland J. Incidence of alcohol and drugs in fatally injured car drivers in Norway. Accident Analysis and Prevention 1993; 25: 479–483.

Glauz WD, Blackburn RR. Drug Use Among Drivers. Report DOT HS 119 2 440. Washington DC: National Highway Traffic Safety Administration, 1975.

Hammersley R, Lavell ET, Forsyth A. Buprenorphine and temazepam abuse. British Journal of Addiction 1990; 85: 301–303.

ILLICIT DRUGS AND DRIVING

Honkanen R, Ertama L, Linoila M, Alha A, Lukkari I, Karlsson M, Kiviluoto O, Puro M. The role of drugs in traffic accidents. British Medical Journal 1980; 281: 1309–1312.

Huizer H. Analytical studies on illicit heroin: II. Comparison of samples. Journal of Forensic Sciences 1983; 28: 44–48.

Hurst PM. Amphetamines and driving. Alcohol, Drugs and Driving 1987; 3: 13–17.

Johnson LD, O'Malley P, Bachman JG. Illicit drug use, smoking and drinking by American high school students, college students and young adults: 1975–1990 Rockville, Maryland: National Institute on Drug Abuse (NIDA), 1990.

Leirer VO, Yesavage JA, Morrow DG. Marijuana carry-over effects on aircraft pilot performance. Aviation, Space and Environmental Medicine 1991; 62:221–227.

Mo BP, Way EL. An assessment of inhalation as a mode of administration of heroin by addicts. The Journal of Pharmacology and Experimental Therapeutics 1966;154:142–151.

Moskowitz H. Marijuana and Driving. Accident Analysis and Prevention 1985; 17:323–345.

Moskowitz H, Robinson CD. Methadone maintenance and tracking performance. In: Kaye S, Meier GW, eds. Alcohol, Drugs and Traffic Safety. Washington: US Department of Transport, 1985:995–1004.

National Institute on Drug Abuse (NIDA). National Household Survey on Drug Abuse 1990 Rockville, Maryland: National Institute on Drug Abuse (NIDA), 1990.

Perera K, Tulley M, Jenner F. The use of benzodiazepines among drug addicts. British Journal of Addiction 1987;82:511–515.

Polkis A, Maginn D, Barr JL. Drug findings in 'driving under the influence of drugs' cases: A problem of illicit drug use. Drug and Alcohol Dependence 1987;20:57–62.

Robinson CD, Moskowitz H. Methadone maintenance treatment and aspects of skilled performance. In: Kaye S, Meier GW, eds. Alcohol, Drugs and Traffic Safety. Washington: US Department of Transport, 1985:1145–1157.

Sakol MS, Stark C, Sykes R. Buprenorphine and temazepam abuse by drug takers in Glasgow: An increase. British Journal of Addiction 1989;84:439–441.

Siegel RK. Cocaine use and driving behaviour. Alcohol, Drugs and Driving 1987;3:1–8.

Smiley AM. Marijuana: On-road and driving simulator studies. Alcohol, Drugs and Driving 1986;2:121–134.

Stoduto G, Viniglis ER, Kapur BM, Sheu W-J, McLellan BA, Liban CB. Alcohol and drug use among motor vehicle collision victims admitted to a Regional Trauma Unit: Demographic, injury and crash characteristics. Accident Analysis and Prevention 1993;25:411–420.

Strang J, Creed F. Confidentiality, driving and the drug addict. Lancet 1984;1:682.

Strang J. New abuse of buprenorphine by snorting. British Medical Journal 1991;302:969.

Strang J, Griffiths P, Abbey J, Gossop M. Survey of use of injected benzodiazepines by drug users in Britain – 1992. British Medical Journal 1994; 308:1082.

Strang J, Griffiths P, Powis B, Gossop M. First use of heroin: Changes in route of administration over time. British Medical Journal 1992;304:1222–1223.

Strang J, Johns A, Caan W. Cocaine in the UK 1991. British Journal of Psychiatry 1993;162:1–13.

Strang J, Ruben S, Farell M, Gossop M. Prescribing heroin and other injectable drugs. In: Strang J, Gossop M, eds. Heroin Addiction and Drug Policy: The British System. Oxford: Oxford University Press, 1994: 192–206.

Strang J, Seivewright N, Farell M. Intravenous and other novel abuses of benzodiazepines: The opening of Pandora's box? British Journal of Addiction 1992;87:1373–1376.

Tennant FS, Rawson RA, Punphrey E, Seecof R. Clinical experiences with 959 opioid-dependent patients treated with Levo-Alpha-Acetylmethadol (LAAM). Journal of Substance Abuse Treatment 1986;3:195–202.

Terhune KW. An evaluation of responsibility analysis for assessing alcohol on drug crash effects. Accident Analysis and Prevention 1983;15:237–246.

Vingilis ER, Stoduto G, Kapur BM, McLellan BA. The role of alcohol and other drugs in seriously injured traffic crash victims. In: Utzelmann H-D, Berghaus G, Kroj G, eds. Alcohol, Drugs and Traffic Safety. Cologne: Verlag TUV Rheinland, 1993:965–71.

Ward J, Mattick R, Hall W. Key Issues in Methadone Maintenance. Kensington: New South Wales University Press, 1992.

ILLICIT DRUGS AND DRIVING

ADDICTION/USE OR DEPENDENCY ON ILLICIT DRUGS*	GROUP I ENTITLEMENT	GROUP II ENTITLEMENT
Cannabis Amphetamines Heroin Morphine Methadone Cocaine LSD/Hallucinogens including misuse of Ecstasy and other psychoactive substances If seizure(s) occur please see under Epilepsy. Applicants or driver on Consultant supervised oral methadone replacement programme may be licensed subject to annual medical review. If on I.V. methadone replacement programme the licence will be recommended to be refused or revoked.	Six months off driving if evidence of Cannabis use. Twelve months off driving is required with other drugs if evidence of dependency or abuse confirmed by urine screening. Till 70 licence will be restored only after satisfactory independent medical examination and negative urine screen for drug abuse. _Patient is recommended to seek help from medical or other agencies during the period off driving, where history indicates drug misuse or dependency._	Recommended refusal or revocation for 3 years, during which no evidence of dependency or continuing misuse must have occurred. On application a Specialist medical examination required with negative urine screen for drugs of abuse.
CHRONIC SOLVENT MISUSE OR DEPENDENCY	Persistent solvent misuse requires driving to cease and DVLA to be notified. Licence would be restored after medical enquiries confirm no continuing misuse.	Recommended refusal or revocation until condition satisfactorily controlled for at least 1 year, with no evidence of continuing misusing or dependency. Specialist medical opinion required.

ILLICIT DRUGS AND DRIVING

ADDICTION/USE OR DEPENDENCY ON ILLICIT DRUGS*	GROUP I ENTITLEMENT	GROUP II ENTITLEMENT
Seizure(s) associated with illicit drug misuse:	With a seizure or seizures associated with illicit drug misuse, a period of 1 year off the road will be required. At the end of that period, before restoration of the licence independent medical evidence will be required, that any previous illicit drug misuse or dependency has ceased. In addition, patients will be assessed as to likely diagnosis of epilepsy.	Barred in law (see Epilepsy).

NB: A Person holding and driving LGV/PCV's, who has been relicensed following illicit drug misuse or dependency must be advised as part of their follow up that if their condition recurs they should cease driving and notify DVLA Medical Branch.

14

ALCOHOL AND DRIVING

Principal Author: Dr Jonathan Chick MA MPhil FRCPE FRCPsych*

The Problem

Alcohol has been identified as an important human factor in road traffic accidents. Simpson and Mayhew (1992) estimate that a 1% 'hard core' of drink-drivers have 200 times the average risk of being involved in a road traffic accident fatality. Drink-drivers may neither be alcohol dependent nor have a disordered personality. However in the United Kingdom as in other countries where research has been carried out, convicted drink drivers tend to be regular heavy drinkers. At least 4% of adults aged 15–65 are dependent on alcohol. Dependence may be chemical and or psychological. A further 4% misuse alcohol at times. Doctors frequently have such individuals under their care, sometimes because of associated medical problems, and many are drivers. Some drivers know their performance is impaired by alcohol, but do not seem to care, but there are those also who genuinely believe their performance is normal or even enhanced when they are intoxicated. Others with an alcohol problem make, and follow sincerely, a rule never to drink and drive. A history of a drink/drive conviction is a pointer, but it is often difficult for the doctor to establish which category his patient falls into. The legal limit when driving is 80mgm/100ml in blood and 35 micrograms per 100ml in breath.

Disclosure to DVLA

Continuing dependence and misuse where the person is likely to drive whilst unfit under the influence of alcohol constitute "relevant and

*   Consultant Psychiatrist, Alcohol Problems Clinic, 35 Morningside Park, Edinburgh EH10 5HD.

prospective disabilities" (Chapter 2, Part 1). The Road Traffic Acts make it an offence if a driving licence holder or applicant fails to notify a relevant disability. At the time of going to press the maximum fine is £1000.

Few patients with alcohol current dependency and misuse fulfil this obligation. Medical practitioners may be failing in their duty of care if they do not alert their patients to the need to notify the Licensing Centre about their condition. Patients should also be advised to inform their motor insurers, because otherwise compensation payments may be refused or compromised. Insurers, however, are unlikely not to honour claims as long as Road Traffic Act and DVLA requirements are satisfied.

Disclosure to DVLA does not necessarily mean suspension of the licence for car and motorcycle drivers, but it usually will in the case of drivers of large goods vehicles and buses. It can, however, lead to an independent medical assessment organised by DVLA, with blood tests. Regular reviews may be recommended. Sometimes this leads to individuals tackling their alcohol problem seriously and successfully perhaps for the first time. Many know that the risks of being caught drinking and driving increase year by year with enhanced police enforcement, as reflected in increasing numbers of breath tests carried out by the police. A problem faced by doctors is that introducing the subject of a "driver notification" may jeopardise a rather delicate doctor/patient relationship.

Sometimes holding a licence is important in the work rehabilitation of a newly abstinent alcoholic. It is important to write to the medical officer in charge of the case at DVLA and seek co-operation. DVLA is entitled by law to grant a licence where the established driving risk is prospective rather than immediate. Often the one year review by DVLA acts as sword of Damocles and helps abstinence compliance.

ALCOHOL AND DRIVING

Since many problem drinkers will not themselves notify DVLA,
the doctor sometimes should do so if he feels the public are at risk,
in accordance with the ethical code of the General Medical Council.
(See Chapter 2) Discussion with another doctor involved with the
patient is often helpful. The family will sometimes make the
notification if advised to do so. In all instances the patient must
be informed, and notes made in the medical case record. If a doctor
failed to take action in a serious case, it could lead to a Civil Action
against him or her for negligence.

Consequences of Drink-Drive Convictions

Treatment of continuing alcohol dependence and misuse is frequently
hampered by the patient's secrecy and even denial. Often doctors face a
dilemma in how to proceed when they strongly suspect such a patient
sometimes drives under the influence. Many such patients do not
appreciate the risks to themselves and the consequences. Driving at a
level of 2½ times the legal limit (200mg of alcohol per 100ml of blood)
increases the risk about 20 times of being involved in a road traffic
accident for the average person. Police officers are empowered to
breathalyse drivers involved in a road traffic accident or where there is
a moving road traffic offence (e.g. non functioning of exterior vehicle
lights after dark or a speeding offence) or where the officer has reason
to believe that a driver has been drinking. A positive roadside screening
result leads to arrest and the requirement to provide an evidential
specimen of breath at a police station using an "evidential" breathalyser
which compares the driver's breath alcohol content against a control
sample of alcohol in helium.

The law provides for tough penalties for those who drink and drive.
The maximum penalty for driving when unfit through drink or drugs

or when over the legal limit is a level 5 fine of £5000, a 6 month prison sentence, plus a disqualification of at least 12 months. The Road Traffic Act 1991 which came into force on 1 July 1992 introduced a new offence of "causing death by careless driving while under the influence of drink or drugs" with a penalty of up to 5 years imprisonment and a disqualification of at least 2 years. This was increased to a maximum of 10 years imprisonment in August 1993. Failure to give a specimen of breath to a police constable results in arrest and the Courts' sentencing regime is usually identical to that of a case where the breath test was over the legal limit. Conviction of a drink-drive offence gives one a criminal record with potential employment consequences. On restoration of the licence after completing the period of ban, motor insurance premiums are usually substantially increased.

Rehabilitation Courses

The Road Traffic Act 1991 provided for a large scale experiment in the use of rehabilitation courses for drink/drive offenders. Such courses have been in use for many years in other countries, such as the United States and Germany. In this country, Magistrates and Sheriffs in selected areas may offer an offender the opportunity of attending a course approved by the Department of Transport. The offender must pay to attend the course, but successful completion of the course entitles the offender to a reduction of up to a quarter in the period of disqualification. The effectiveness of the courses in changing attitudes and preventing reoffending is being monitored and the Act provides for the introduction of legislation for the future nationwide extension of the scheme. Health professionals are sometimes involved in either organising these courses or speaking at particular sessions. Similar rehabilitation courses are run by Probation Services in some areas, but these are usually for offenders who might otherwise have been at risk of a custodial sentence and are served as a condition of a probation order. Failure to comply with this order will mean that the offender is committed to the Court for resentencing.

The High Risk Offender Scheme

Conviction of a drink-drive offence may lead to some drivers being categorised as high risk offenders. This means that before their licence is restored to them, after serving their period of disqualification, they have to undergo a medical assessment to ensure they are not continuing to misuse alcohol. Any of the following define an offender as "high risk":

- One disqualification for drink driving when the level of alcohol is 2¹/₂ times or more the legal limit (i.e. 200mg of alcohol per 100ml of blood).

- One disqualification due to failing to provide, without reasonable excuse, a specimen for analysis.

- Two disqualifications or more within ten years for being unfit through drink, or for driving when the level of alcohol exceeds the legal limit.

At the time of conviction DVLA writes to them informing them that they should reapply for their driving licence at least three months before the period of their disqualification from driving ends. They are recommended to seek help from their doctors or alcohol treatment agencies if they consider they have a drink problem. They are told that on reapplication for their licence, they will be subject to blood tests. Where the result suggest possible continued drinking they are medically examined. If this examination shows evidence of continuing excessive drinking, then the application to renew the licence is refused on grounds that driving would be likely to be a source of danger to the public. These cases are invited to reapply in six months time when the tests are repeated but they may reapply whenever they so choose. If the blood tests or medical examination first initiated shows no evidence of alcohol dependence or misuse then the till 70 driving licence entitlement is restored, or where the person is over 70 the three year licence entitlement restored. If however, the result of the test is borderline, then a one year licence is issued and the test repeated annually for a reasonable period after which, if there is no further evidence of continuing dependence or recurrent misuse, the full driving entitlement will be restored.

Group II Driving

As stated in the EU Directive above, drivers who misuse alcohol have to meet more stringent legal requirements if they wish to drive goods vehicles or buses (Group II standards). The DVLA follows the recommendations of the Royal College of Psychiatrists (1993) regarding drivers of LGV and PCV's. These are:

"Dependence on alcohol or continuing chronic alcohol consumption with inability to refrain from drinking and driving and drug abuse with dependence on psychotropic substances should lead to advice to the patient to inform the DVLA and discontinue driving in the meantime. After a three year period of abstinence from alcohol and subject to authorised medical opinion and regular medical check-ups, the EU Directive 91/439 allows the issue or renewal of a licence for applicants or drivers who have in the past been dependent on alcohol."

Doctors glad to see a patient recovering from alcohol dependence have sometimes found the three year period of confirmed abstinence prior to licence renewal harsh. However, the recommendation is based on the high relapse rate in patients recovering from alcohol dependence for at least the first two years. This period is justified by the higher road traffic risks to the public in the case of accidents involving large goods and passenger carrying vehicles. Large goods vehicles have approximately three times the average road traffic accident fatality rate per mile travelled and buses three to four times the average rate. This is largely due to the size of the vehicles and also the fact that buses operate most frequently in urban and city areas, where there are greater numbers of road users.

Medical Assessment for alcohol dependence or misuse

In clinical practice, the diagnosis of alcohol dependence or current misuse usually relies on information revealed by the patient or family. However, the Medical Advisers of the DVLA have understandably sought to use more objective markers. No single blood test marker has sufficient accuracy. At the time of writing the interpretation of the existing blood test markers (liver enzymes and MCV) is the subject of a study by the Royal College of Pathologists and a newer blood test marker (carbohydrate deficient transferring) is showing promising specificity. A detailed clinical drinking or drug history, with the help if necessary of the subject's general practitioner, ensures false positives are extremely few.

Where a person complains to DVLA claiming that they are the victim of a false positive assessment, the Agency may arrange a further and full assessment, but whatever that result, at the end of the day the individual has a right to take his case to a Magistrates' Court in England and Wales or the Sheriff's in Scotland.

ALCOHOL AND DRIVING

Advice to Patients

Patients who are dependent on alcohol or unable to refrain from drinking and driving must be advised to stop driving, and notify the DVLA, Swansea. (See Chapter II Part 2 if the advice is rejected). Patients who have lost their licences on the grounds of an alcohol problem, or are high risk offenders, should be advised to seek medical help, be subject to 6–8 weekly serum liver enzyme and MVC measurements over the next year or more, to confirm they have attained abstinence (or occasionally if their doctor or specialist agrees, a return to very limited social drinking).

REFERENCES

Allen JP, Litten RZ, Anton RF, Cross GM (1994) Carbohydrate – deficient transferring as a measure of immoderate drinking: remaining issues. Alcoholism: Clinical and Experimental Research, 18, 799–812.

Royal College of Psychiatrists (1993) Psychiatric Standards of fitness to drive large goods vehicles (LGV's) and passenger carrying vehicles (PCV's) **Psychiatric Bulletin**, 17, 631–2

Simpson H M, Mayhew D R 1992 – The Hard Core Drink Driver, Traffic Injury Research Foundation, Toronto, Canada

Appendix – Definitions of alcohol misuse and dependence.

World Health Organisation: ICD-10.

Harmful use: "A pattern of alcohol use that is causing damage to health, either physical or mental." Dependence: "Three or more of the following in the previous year: a strong desire or sense of compulsion to take alcohol; difficulty in controlling drinking; withdrawal symptoms; increased tolerance; neglect of interests and/or spending more time on obtaining alcohol; persistent drinking despite knowledge of harm".

ALCOHOL AND DRIVING

ALCOHOL PROBLEMS	GROUP I ENTITLEMENT	GROUP II ENTITLEMENT
ALCOHOL MISUSE/ABUSE ALCOHOL DEPENDENCY There is no single definition which embraces all the variables in these conditions. But as a guideline the following is offered: "a state which because of consumption of alcohol, causes disturbance of behaviour, related disease or other consequences, likely to cause the patient, his family or society harm now or in the future and which may or may not be associated with dependency. In addition assessment of the alcohol consumption with respect to current national advised guidelines is necessary."	After medical confirmation and/or examination licence recommended to be refused or revoked for at least 6 months freedom from misuse/abuse has been attained, or at least 1 year freedom from dependency or detoxification. Independent medical examination arranged by DVLA with confirmation of satisfactory liver enzyme tests and MCV, with if necessary medical report from own doctors, before the licence is restored. Patient recommended to seek help from medical or other sources during the period off the road.	Recommended refusal or revocation for 3 years, during which there should be evidence that no dependency or continued misuse has occurred. On reapplication examination by a Consultant with a special interest in alcohol abuse will be required, with confirmation of satisfactory liver enzyme tests and MCV. If seizure or seizures have occurred, the vocational Epilepsy Regulations apply (see Epilepsy).
* Seizure(s) associated with or withdrawal from alcohol, in addition patients will be assessed as to the likely diagnosis of epilepsy.	With a seizure or seizures associated with alcohol, a period of 1 year off the road will be required. Before restoration of the licence, medical evidence will be required, that previous alcohol misuse or dependency has ceased.	Epilepsy Group II regulations may apply, see Chapter 6.

ALCOHOL AND DRIVING

ALCOHOL PROBLEMS	GROUP I ENTITLEMENT	GROUP II ENTITLEMENT
ACUTE/CHRONIC ALCOHOL RELATED DISORDERS e.g. severe hepatic cirrhosis, Wernicke's encephalopathy, Korsakoffs Psychosis, acute alcohol detoxification et alia.	Recommended to be refused/revoked.	Recommended to be refused/revoked.

NB: A person holding and driving LGV/PVC's, who has been relicensed following alcohol misuse or dependency must be advised as part of their follow up that if their condition recurs they should cease driving and notify DVLA Medical Branch.

HIGH RISK OFFENDER SCHEME for drivers convicted of certain drink/driving offences

1. One disqualification or more for drink/driving when the level of alcohol is 2½ or more times the legal limit.

2. One disqualification or more that he/she failed, without reasonable excuse to provide a specimen for analysis.

3. Two disqualifications or more within 10 years for being unfit through drink.

4. Two disqualifications or more within 10 years when the level of alcohol exceeds the legal limit.

DVLA will be notified by courts. On application for a licence satisfactory liver enzyme and MCV tests will be required and follow up medical examinations organised. If the result is favourable the till 70 licence is restored for Group I and any Group II entitlement included.

If High Risk Offender associated with previous history of alcohol dependency or misuse, after above satisfactory examination and blood tests, short period licence only for ordinary and vocational issued, depending on time interval between previous history and reapplication.

High Risk Offender found to have current unfavourable alcohol misuse history and/or abnormal blood test analysis would have application refused.

15

MISCELLANEOUS DISORDERS

Chronic renal failure

Achieving medical fitness depends on meeting the fitness standards in the individual chapters of this book. In the case of recurrent uraemic symptomatic epilepsy, the epilepsy regulations apply (see Chapter 6). A person who is receiving continuous ambulatory peritoneal dialysis or haemo-dialysis who is asymptomatic is permitted to hold a licence until the age of 70. Group II drivers are individually assessed by DVLA medical branch.

Renal transplant recipients

Group I are licensed until the age of 70 providing they are asymptomatic whilst **Group II** drivers retain their entitlement subject to annual review.

Aids Syndrome

HIV positive people need not notify DVLA.

Symptomatic aids syndrome cases may continue to drive providing they are able to meet the fitness standards in the individual chapters of this book.

Malignant tumours metastasising to the brain

For **Group I** DVLA must be notified and driving cease if cerebral secondaries are present, in view of the risk of epilepsy.

Group II driving should stop for two years from the time of diagnosis of the primary tumour and driving is then permitted providing treatment is satisfactory and there is no brain scan evidence of intracranial metastatic deposits.

ANNEX I
DRIVING ASSESSMENT FOR PERSONS WITH PHYSICAL DISABILITIES

Medical Practitioners dealing with disabled persons will wish to be aware of their needs for mobility.

It is advisable for a disabled person who wants to learn to drive, or who is returning to driving with a new or ongoing disability, to have an assessment of driving ability and/or advice on the sort of controls and equipment needed to overcome any physical limitations. The Licensing Centre in Swansea may, depending on the nature of the disability, restrict the licence to vehicles "fitted with controls to suit the disability". Clearly the cost of such adaptations will be important in making a decision about vehicle modifications. There is a no need to notify DVLA of a static non progressive disability unless adaptation to the vehicle (including automatic transmission)is required. For Group II entitlement significant physical disability may result in refusal or revocation.

NB: A person in receipt of mobility allowance may hold a driving licence from 16 years of age.

The four main groups of impairment which may influence the ability to drive or the need for modifications to vehicles are:

1) Limb Disabilities: (upper or lower, partial or complete)

   e.g. Amputation, limb deformity, joint restriction, muscular impairment.

2) Spinal Disabilities:

   e.g. Paraparesis or Tetraparesis, deformity pain.

   e.g. Traumatic/Spondylitis/ Spondylosis.

DRIVING ASSESSMENT FOR PERSONS WITH PHYSICAL DISABILITIES

3) General or specific impairment of ability to control because of weakness impaired mobility etc.

e.g. From injury or illness. e.g. chronic neurological disorders.

Adaptations needed may include:

Automatic transmission, power assisted steering, hand controls to accelerate and brake, left foot accelerator pedal, joy stick control/tiller control, adaptations to secondary controls, steering aids, adaptations to handbrake and gear selector, special mirrors, seat belt modifications, special seating, wheelchair stowage equipment, infra red remote control systems. It is important to recognise that the technology to modify vehicles suitable for disabled drivers is improving rapidly. In addition the disabled driver should be aware of the Motability organisation who provide useful information about financial measures to assist in purchasing or modifying vehicles for the disabled.

4) Impairment of cognitive function

e.g. post stroke, post head injury, early dementia

There is no single or simple marker for assessment of impaired cognitive function although the ability to manage satisfactorily unassisted day to day living is a reasonable yardstick of cognitive competence. When recovery is complete clinically, in car assessment on the road with a valid Licence or on private motor circuits without a valid licence are an invaluable method of ensuring that there are no features present which are liable to be a source of danger e.g. visual inattention, easy distractibility, difficulty performing multiple tasks and driving at speed. In addition it is implicit that reaction time, memory, concentration and confidence are adequate and do not show impairment likely to affect driving performance.

DRIVING ASSESSMENT FOR PERSONS WITH PHYSICAL DISABILITIES

Driving Assessment Centres exist in various parts of the country offering advice on all aspects of transport and disability. A list of Assessment Centres is attached but further Centres are being developed.

An information pack is available from MAVIS, Department of Transport, TRL Crowthorne, Berks RG11 6AU (Telephone 0344-770456). Other Centres have similar information packs and the nearest Centre would be happy to give general information or specific advice with regard to driving and other mobility problems.

FORUM DISABLED DRIVERS' ASSESSMENT CENTRES

BANSTEAD MOBILITY CENTRE

Damson Way, Orchard Hill
Queen Mary's Avenue
Carshalton, Surrey SM5 4NR
Tel: 0181 770 1151
Fax: 0181 770 1211

CORNWALL FRIENDS
MOBILITY CENTRE

Tehidy House, Treliske Hospital
Truro, Cornwall TR1 3LJ
Tel: 01782 206060

DERBY DISABLED
DRIVING CENTRE

Kingsway Hospital
Kingsway, Derby DE3 3LZ
Tel: 01332 371929

DISABILITY ACTION
(no Medical Practitioner)

2 Annadale Avenue
Belfast BT7 3UR
Tel: 01232 491011

EDINBURGH DRIVING
ASSESSMENT SERVICE
MOBILITY CENTRE

Astley Ainslie Hospital
133 Grange Loan
Edinburgh EH9 2HL
Tel: 0131 5379192

DRIVING ASSESSMENT FOR PERSONS WITH PHYSICAL DISABILITIES

KILVERSTONE
MOBILITY CENTRE

Kilverstone Country Park
Kilverstone, Thetford
Norfolk IP24 2RL
Tel: 01842 75302

MOBILITY ADVICE AND
VEHICLE INFORMATION
SERVICE (MAVIS)

Department of Transport
TRL Crowthorne
Berkshire RG11 6AU
Tel: 01344 770456
Fax: 01344 770356

MOBILITY CENTRE
HUNTERS MOOR

Regional Rehabilitation Centre
Hunters Road
Newcastle upon Tyne NE2 4NR
Tel: 0191 221 0454

MOBILITY INFORMATION
SERVICE
(No Medical Practitioner)

Unit 2A, Atcham Estate
Upton Magna
Shrewsbury SY4 4UG
Tel: 01743 761889

WRIGHTINGTON MOBILITY
CENTRE

Wrightington Hospital
Hall Lane, Wrightington
Wigan, Lancs WD6 3EP
Tel: 01257 256280Y

All these centres have modified cars and are able to undertake in – car assessments

DRIVING ASSESSMENT FOR PERSONS WITH PHYSICAL DISABILITIES

ADDITIONAL DRIVER ASSESSMENT CENTRES

CLATTERBRIDGE DRIVING
ASSESSMENT CENTRE FOR
THE DISABLED

Clatterbridge Hospital
Bebington, Wirral
Merseyside L63 4JY
Tel: 0151 334 4000

DEVON DRIVERS'
ASSESSMENT CENTRE

Westpoint, Clyst St Mary
Exeter
Tel: 01392 444773

DRIVING ASSESSMENT CENTRE

Mary Marlborough Lodge
Nuffield Orthopaedic Centre
NHS Trust, Windmill Road
Headington, Oxford OX3 7LD
Tel: 01865 227449

REGIONAL REHABILITATION
CENTRE

Mobility Centre
South Birmingham Health Authority
Oaktree Lane, Selly Oak
Birmingham B29 6J
Tel: 0121 627 8221

ROOKWOOD HOSPITAL

Llandaff, Cardiff CF5 2NY
Tel: 01222 566281

WALES DISABLED DRIVERS
ASSESSMENT CENTRE

18 Plas Newydd, Whitchurch
Cardiff CF4 1NR
Tel: 01222 615276

ANNEX II
MEDICAL EXEMPTION FROM SEATBELT WEARING

The law allows exemption from seatbelt wearing on medical grounds. Exemptions granted should take due account of the evidence showing seatbelt wearing reduces the risk of injury or death in road accidents. A range of devices can be used to overcome difficulties experienced, especially by disabled people. Temporary certificates can be issued. Patients refused exemption can request a second opinion from another medical practitioner.

The Road Traffic Act 1988 and regulations made under it, require drivers and passengers in motor vehicles to wear seatbelts, subject to certain exemptions.

One exemption applies to "any person holding a valid certificate signed by a medical practitioner to the effect that it is inadvisable on medical grounds for him to wear and seatbelt".

There is overwhelming evidence that wearing front and rear seatbelts substantially reduces the number of deaths and disabling injuries in accidents involving vehicle occupants.

Taking all types of injury, including fatalities, reductions of up to 50% have been recorded. Injuries to the head, face and eyes are particularly reduced.

Medical practitioners, therefore need to balance very carefully the advantage to their patient reducing the risk of serious injury or death against any reason a patient has for seeking exemption from wearing a seatbelt.

Should a patient granted exemption be injured in a road traffic accident, as a result of not wearing a belt, the possibility of a civil law

MEDICAL EXEMPTION FROM
SEATBELT WEARING

claim for negligence against a doctor cannot be ruled out.

It is important to assess patients thoroughly, whenever possible asking for a demonstration in the vehicle of the difficulty experienced.

A record should be kept of exemptions issued.

Disabled Patients

Most disabled people can and do wear belts without undue discomfort or inconvenience. A comparatively small number experience difficulties, many of which can be easily resolved by simple measures such as the following:

"Drop Links" designed to lower the position of the belt and alter the lay of the diagonal. This is particularly useful for people of restricted growth, where the conventional diagonal would otherwise cross the neck.

"Pulla Belts" a simple sleeve addition to the belt for people who cannot reach the top anchorage point to pull the conventional belt across them.

"The Clever Clip" designed to ease belt tension across the chest and reduce any restriction of breathing. It can also reduce pressure on the abdomen, for instance for patients with a colostomy.

A survey for the Royal Association for Disability and Rehabilitation (RADAR) on behalf of the Department of Transport, showed that 3/4 of the difficulties with seatbelts encountered by disabled people could be resolved by these solutions.

Further advice for disabled patients is available from RADAR, 25 Mortimer Street, London W1N 8AB, telephone no. 0171 637 5400.

MEDICAL EXEMPTION FROM SEATBELT WEARING

MAVIS Transport Research Laboratory, Crowthorne, Berkshire RG11 6AU, telephone no. 0344 770456.

Duration of medical exemption certificates

All certificates must now specify the period of validity. The period may be as long or as short as the medical practitioner considers justifiable.

Validity of old style certificates

Certificates issued for an unlimited period on the old style forms will continue to be valid indefinitely. Unused stocks of these forms may be issued up to 31 December 1994 but no later.

It should be noted that they do not bear the EEC symbol and will not be recognised in EEC member states other than in the UK. Some holders of these forms, may therefore wish to have a new certificate issued. They should be asked to surrender their old form.

Refusals

If people are refused exemption, it is important that they are given a clear reason. If they are not satisfied, they may, on payment obtain a second opinion from another registered medical practitioner.

Supplies of seatbelt exemption certificates are obtainable on writing to:

"Health Publications Unit"
No 2 Site
Manchester Road
Haywood
Lancashire OL10 2P2

The letter should quote reference no. FPN318.

ANNEX III

OLDER DRIVERS –
GENERAL INFORMATION

CONDENSED FROM "HELPING THE OLDER DRIVER" THE REPORT OF AN AA/MCAP WORKING GROUP

As people become older they will seek advice on how to adapt their driving to take account of their general fitness. The information that follows is designed to help older people to adapt their driving habits and lifestyle to the limitations posed by their increasing age, and to prepare for the day when they may have to give up driving.

Older drivers should be aware that ability will decline, although some may wish to deny that this is so. Decline in ability does not mean stopping driving, but recognition of decline should lead to an acceptance of the situation, positive adjustment, and less worry.

The ability to recognise causes of tension, or that tension is in fact occurring when driving, is important so that older drivers may continue to drive safely and comfortably. If tension is not countered, driving is likely to be reduced, and end, sooner than might otherwise be necessary.

Choice of Car and Equipment

Older drivers need a good field of vision requiring minimum movement of the head. Adequate mirrors and clear glass giving all-round vision (particularly for reversing) are essential requirements for older drivers.

The use of "Blind spot" wedge-shaped, supplementary rear view mirrors is highly recommended, since the older person often has a limited range of head movement.

Glasses used for driving should not have thick frames and side-pieces which obscure vital peripheral vision.

Any transfer from a manual to an automatic gearbox, or to power steering should not be left too late, as some drivers may not readily adapt, particularly in an emergency.

Planning Journeys

Older drivers are happiest driving on roads they use regularly, and planning these routes can pay dividends. A route using mainly left turns is safer.

Older drivers can have trouble interpreting direction signs in busy or complicated traffic situations, creating navigation problems. A prepared route with place names, road and junction numbers can help, leaving little information to be obtained from signs. Passengers can help with directions, leaving the driver to concentrate on the driving.

Extreme weather, be it rain, fog, ice or snow makes travel less safe, and more stressful. Most trips can be cancelled under these conditions. Trips to the shops can always be postponed for a few days. In very bad weather all drivers should only travel if the journey is essential.

Many older drivers prefer not to drive in the dark, finding it harder to understand complex traffic situations, and to read traffic signs.

Many feel that the problems of glare and dazzle increase with age. The effect of glare can be diminished by keeping the windscreen clean as smears and smudges decrease visibility. When driving against bright light such blemishes can make a windscreen almost opaque.

If an older driver finds night driving difficult or worrying he or she should not drive at night.

Older Drivers – General Information

Peak hours in towns are easy to anticipate, although they tend to start early on Fridays. Long distance motorway commuting also takes place at these times. Similarly, heavy traffic can be anticipated at weekends and Bank Holidays, and much weekend traffic now travels on Friday evenings.

Traffic and weather information is available on radio, Teletext, in the papers and through recorded telephone messages. This information, can identify problems and remove much of the worry from driving.

Avoidance of Fatigue

Drowsiness at the wheel is common among older drivers and is exacerbated by alcohol and some medicines. Adequate ventilation in the car helps prevent drowsiness.

Fatigue is best avoided by advance planning. It is important to have adequate sleep before travelling and to avoid heavy meals and alcohol. Setting out early in the day is better than late and journeys should not be started after strenuous muscular activity. Driving should be avoided at times when the driver either is, or might become, fatigued, and at times when he or she might otherwise be sleeping.

A trip should not involve driving for more than six hours a day, and breaks should be taken at least every two hours. Frequent breaks are best, and these should be for at least twenty minutes. A change of driver can be a good idea.

If a driver feels tired during a journey a stop should be made at the first possible opportunity.

Driving on strange roads is tiring. But the danger may well come at the end of a journey, when familiar territory is reached. At this point the driver may relax, and 'nodding off' can easily follow.

OLDER DRIVERS –
GENERAL INFORMATION

Medication and Alcohol

Surveys of drivers have indicated a disturbing lack of knowledge of the adverse effects of drugs on driving and claims that doctors often provide no information.

Alcohol and ageing have a similar effect on the processing of information by a driver. The older driver, needs to be particularly alert to the effects of alcohol.

It is important that doctors assume that all older people drive and when prescribing medication advise the patient about side-effects that may affect driving ability. Patients should be told not to drive if the side-effects occur, and not to stop taking the medication in order to drive. Similarly they must be told that with many drugs alcohol increases side-effects, and it is inadvisable to drive after drinking anything alcoholic. The combination of drink, medicines and driving should be avoided at all costs.

Giving up driving

Research has shown that many older people are almost totally dependent on the car for the maintenance of their lifestyles – especially with the decline of local bus and train services, local post offices and the movement of shops and hospitals to out-of-town locations. Yet for many the day will come when they, or their spouses, have to give up driving.

It is important that older people plan for this event. This planning can start ahead of retirement, particularly if it is intended to move house. Access to those facilities that older people need (doctors, hospitals, shops, friends and relatives) must be possible without a car.